T0082918

The Letter

Reflections of a high school swim coach

Brad Fleener

authorHOUSE®

AuthorHouse™
1663 Liberty Drive
Bloomington, IN 47403
www.authorhouse.com
Phone: 833-262-8899

© 2021 Brad Fleener. All rights reserved.

No part of this book may be reproduced, stored in a retrieval system, or
transmitted by any means without the written permission of the author.

Published by AuthorHouse 07/06/2021

ISBN: 978-1-6655-3108-5 (sc)
ISBN: 978-1-6655-3107-8 (e)

Print information available on the last page.

Any people depicted in stock imagery provided by Getty Images are models,
and such images are being used for illustrative purposes only.
Certain stock imagery © Getty Images.

This book is printed on acid-free paper.

Because of the dynamic nature of the Internet, any web addresses or
links contained in this book may have changed since publication and
may no longer be valid. The views expressed in this work are solely those
of the author and do not necessarily reflect the views of the publisher,
and the publisher hereby disclaims any responsibility for them.

This book is dedicated to the hundreds of student athletes who inspired me daily, taught me more than I taught them, and believed in my methods.

Special thanks to all the coaches who worked with me. Especially Marie Mittmann-Guerrero who, besides sharing the same home state and birthday, was MY first swim coach.

Introduction

I grew up playing sports, the standard baseball, basketball, and football. Mix in skiing, motorcycles, and raging ping pong games with my brothers and you get the idea that sports were an important part of my life. I considered myself fairly athletic. Of all the sports, baseball was the one that stuck. The one I eventually played in college. Feeling the need to fuel my competitive fire after college, I started racing triathlons. That passion became a short-lived profession. All the while I was still in search of my ultimate goal, teaching PE and coaching baseball. My first teaching job was at a middle school in Palm Springs, CA. It took me one year to realize I didn't want to teach PE. I needed a little more mental stimulation. During my 2nd year of teaching a woman saw me training at the local community pool and asked if I ever thought about coaching swim. Apparently, the local club team was in search of a coach. I told her I had never coached swimming or considered coaching swimming. She said the team was small and in transition and that I would be a great fit. I hesitantly agreed, knowing nothing about age-group swimming. A few years of that proved unsatisfying so I stopped.

A friend of mine had just become the Athletic Director at a new high school and asked if I'd be interested in coaching the swim team. He said the school had no pool and only a few swimmers, none of which were that good. For some reason, I took the position. Long story short, that job changed my life.

Growing up as an athlete, my life was not littered with memorable coaches in any sport. I didn't have many who did more than just manage practices and games. A few were sincere and tried their best to teach and motivate. My fondest memories were of my 6th grade flag football coach. We never lost a game. Mostly because when we won we all got Slurpees from 7 Eleven. Now that is motivation!

When I began coaching High School swim in 1992, I really only had two goals for my athletes; have fun and improve. For me, it was always more than just performance and results. Five, ten, twenty years from now, would they look back at their high school athletic experience and smile? Would they share stories with friends? Would they even remember the coach or any of their teammates? Knowing that many would never swim beyond high school, I wanted to make sure they could answer each of those questions with a resounding YES. I am so thankful for the blind faith my athletes had in me those first few years. The expression, "fake it until you make it" could not have been more appropriate. It was literally day to day for me. My goal was to try my best to make them want to come back each day. That led to a number of traditions we carried on until the day I stopped coaching in 2019. One of the traditions I started in 2001 was writing personal letters to all seniors and sharing those letters at our season-ending awards night. It didn't matter if they swam one year or four. My thought was, they had put in so much work and sacrifice to swim for me, that writing them a personal letter seemed only appropriate. (side note: see 2001 'day in the life' to get an idea of what my athletes had to endure). I quickly found out while trying to read these letters through tears to that first group in 2001, that future letters had to be read by one of my other coaches. If I was going to cry again, and I did, it would be while writing these letters in my home office. I only wish I had started writing letters when I began coaching. An incredible history was established by some amazing student-athletes from 1992 to 2000. I have since gone back and written a few letters to kids in those eras and will continue to do so. The following letters are a tribute to those student-athletes who changed my life.

* Each year begins with a year-end review. You will get a small glimpse of the uniqueness of the program.

Chapter One

2001

Dear Friend,

It is once again my pleasure and privilege to share with you some of the memories of this past 2001 Cathedral City Swim season. I am happy and humbled at the triumphs of the past 3 ½ months. I am also reminded of a friend of mine who, 9 years ago, after hearing I was going to take this swim job at Cathedral City High School, laughing questioned my sanity in stepping into a "no-win situation." At the time I had to agree and 9 years later I still, in some ways, agree with his assessment. We have no reason and every excuse not to be successful. We have no budget to speak of, we have no facilities, we have no wealth of experienced club swimmers to draw from, we have horrible practice times available to us, and we are not well known in the valley. What we do have is heart, determination, desire, supportive parents and families, kids willing to do whatever is necessary, spirit, enthusiasm, and character. Someone once said, "The harder I work the luckier I get." Well, we must be the luckiest swim team around because I don't believe anyone has to make more of a commitment than our athletes do to be called swimmers at Cathedral City.

A typical day in the life of a Varsity Swimmer At Cathedral City High School

- *4:30am - Wake up*
- *5-6:30am - Practice*
- *7:10am - Breakfast in room 210*
- *7:30am-2:21pm - School*
- *2:30pm-3:20pm - Study Hall*
- *3:30pm - Catch school bus to Palm Springs Swim Center*
- *4pm-6:30pm - Practice*
- *7pm - Arrive by bus back to school*

Could you? Would you? Swimmers at Cathedral City have been doing this for 9 years. We've never known any other way. Talent, or lack thereof, has had very little to do with our success. The commitment our athletes make on a daily basis has had everything to do with our success.

*The 2001 Swim Team has written its own chapter. Both Varsity and JV Girls repeated as League Champions. Cathedral City Varsity swimmers won 7 of 11 girls events at the Desert Valley League Championships. Seven girls and one boy represented the Lions at CIF with the girls placing 8th and our "one man" team placing 30th out of 36 qualifying teams. The girls have placed in the Top Ten at CIF in 6 of their 9 seasons. The girls have **not** had a CIF finalist only once. Two school records and six class records fell. Ashley H, who will attend Cal State-Northridge on a Swim & Water Polo Scholarship in the Fall, broke Leslie H's (UCLA) School Record in the 50 Free (24.41) while Adam K broke the records held by Brad M (Cal State-Bakersfield) in the 50 Free (22.32) and 100 Fly (58.65). Adam also broke Brad's Junior class records in the Fly, 100 Free (49.20) and 50 Free (22.32). Freshman Jillian F also broke class records set by Lyndee H (UCLA) in the 100 Back (1:04.18) and, 100 Fly (1:00.53).*

The Varsity Girls were led by Ashley H. (DVL Champion in the 50 & 100 Free, 5th & 6th in those events at CIF) and Seniors Liz Z. (3rd in DVL in

3

the 500 Free and 100 Back), Lorelle H (DVL 100 Breaststroke Champion and 16th at CIF, 3rd in 100 fly at DVL), Junior Alexis F, (16th at CIF and 3rd at DVL in the 50 Free, and 2nd in the 100 Breast at DVL) and Freshman Jillian F (DVL Champion 100 Fly & 200 IM, 6th at CIF in 200 IM and 12th in the 100 Fly). They recorded 10 wins against 2 losses and went undefeated in league for the 5th time to capture their 5th DVL Championship in the last 7 years.

The JV Girls also went 10-2 overall and 6-1 in league to also win their 5th Championship. Their enthusiasm and energy more than made up for their lack of experience. By the end of the season, their time drops were phenomenal. The team was made of primarily Freshmen and Sophomores with little or no swim experience. It is extremely rewarding to see them do so well after working so hard. They learn early the good news and bad news about swimming at Cathedral City. The good news is they are treated the same as Varsity swimmers, they are given the same attention with the same expectations. The bad news is that they are treated like Varsity swimmers. This is difficult for some to understand, but when they finally get it, they reap the benefits of their dedication.

The Boys team suffered a similar fate in terms of numbers. Seven boys were called a team and only four had previous swimming experience. Wins and losses were not a true representation of their dedication and achievement. Adam K. continued his assault on the record books, most of which are or were held by Brad M. '96. Juniors Eric R and Chris C as well as Sophomore Martin S continued their steady improvement. First-year swimmers Tyler C, Andres C, and Cory A, all had tremendous seasons. All three made it to DVL Finals in their respective events.

Another Spring Break, another Spring Trip. A record was definitely set for distance traveled. Cocoa Beach, Florida marked the farthest destination of any trip we've taken. It began with an ominous flight to what we thought would be Denver, Colorado. Clouds and fog prevented us from landing and we were sent to Colorado Springs to land and refuel before going on to Denver. Incredible winds, reaching 100 mph, made it the bumpiest flight this coach has ever been on. That sentiment was echoed by many of the swimmers, some of whom were flying for the first time. It felt more like the roller coaster ride we would later experience at Universal Studios Islands of Adventure than a plane flight. Needless to say many people on the plane, including our own "Ms K", had trouble holding down breakfast. We were never so happy to be on the earth again.

The week was spent, as usual, working very hard swimming twice a day at a local community college. Most of our meals were eaten at the Cocoa Sports Expo, a former major league spring training facility for the Detroit Tigers. Many other teams (no swim teams) were also using the facilities. Many were baseball teams, but there were also a few lacrosse teams training. This naturally prompted comments from our swimmers like, "What are they doing?" "Is that a sport?" and "Why are they wearing skirts?" Naturally, a few days were spent refreshing ourselves in the <u>warm</u> Atlantic Ocean. The surprise of the week was an airboat ride through the Florida Everglades, complete with Alligator sightings. Those creatures are big and strange looking!

The "Titusville Police" took top honors in the traditional weeklong team competitions. One of the highlights of the week was the "best pick up line" competition. Lines like "Are you tired? Because you've been running through my mind all day" or "Do you have 35 cents? My mom told me to call her when I met the woman of my dreams." Cheesy yes, but very hilarious! Universal Studios the last day *was a welcome change of pace. The water rides were well attended as the weather wasn't much different than home.*

My goal as coach remains the same. Work hard, have fun, see what happens. While most teams in other sports experience what they feel is a "long" season, our kids feel like the season comes and goes all too quickly. The week after the season ends is often the longest week of the year for them. They generally don't know what to do with themselves. Memories are constantly being made and barriers are being broken. Traditions are sternly maintained and history is forever being written. I can think of nothing more satisfying than kids who have story after story to tell of their experiences as swimmers at Cathedral City. Thank you for contributing to the memory.

Swimmingly

❖ The Exchange ❖
Jessica P

In what has developed into one of many traditions, I wait in September for the latest foreign exchange student to enter my room choosing to swim. Last Fall, a tall, red-haired girl walked in and said "Are you the swim coach?" as if my white face and non-swimmer build didn't give it away, "Yes," I said, to which she responded, "My name is Jessica and I am from Germany."

The rest, as they say, is history. Jessica, you have the curse of ultimately becoming known as the country you are from. This is also a tradition. I believe you picked water polo and swimming with no idea of what you were getting yourself into. Immersing yourself in the culture is one thing, immersing yourself at 5 am is another. I believe your words were "Are you serious?" These three small words would echo throughout the year. For variety's sake, you would sometimes utter, "You can't be serious?" I was amazed at how quickly you learned each sport and how, my expectations, and to interact with the other athletes. You also learned to pick up the ins and outs of each sport. You not only learned two sports; you learned them well.

Your sense of humor is one of your most endearing qualities. You have this ability to introduce humor into a situation at just the right time, often at your own expense. Whether it is letting a ball bounce off your head, accidentally of course, or doing zipper when every other swimmer is doing catch up, you never seemed to be overcome by the situation.

I hope that, as you return home to your family, you will return with many fond memories. That you will sit at the table with them and share stories about this past year. Stories about practice, stories about bus rides, stories about water polo games, stories about laughter, stories about Florida, and stories about the friends you have made.

Thank you for making this year special for many. You will always be remembered.

fleen

❖ **The Determined** ❖
Kelly G

What do you say about someone who just couldn't manage to stay healthy? You had more than your share of drama this year. How one season could have so many ups and downs is beyond me. Coming into the season I think we both had a much different picture of how the season would progress. I envisioned tremendous improvement in what had been an outstanding first season of swimming as a Junior. Your natural ability carried you to some incredible times last year.

Then your Senior year began. After many weeks of uncertainty, what was once a mystery soon became clear, pneumonia. There are many times that things happen to us in life that we cannot explain. The question at that point was not why, but what. What do I do now?

You had every reason to stop swimming and not many to continue. There isn't a worse feeling than not being able to do what you used to do. What I admire about you is your desire to persevere. Your determination to want to be better. Your willingness to continue.

When many would have thrown in the towel, you didn't. I believe that makes a more profound statement about your accomplishments this season than any time in the 50 or 100 free ever would.

When you look back at your senior year, I hope it is with fond memories. Not memories about how fast or slow you went, but about how you did what you could to the best of your ability. Your example was not lost on the other swimmers.

Thank you for contributing to this season in so many ways.

fleen

❖ **The Gift** ❖
Lorelle H

It's not normal to meet the type of people I often hear about. You know, the type who has never met a situation they didn't like, even if it's the epicenter of the earthquake, the eye of the hurricane, or the center of the storm. Things have never been calm around you as long as I have known you. And that's been a long time. I'm convinced you have a gene that, as you say, "turns people's frowns upside down." I'm convinced you have no concept of public volume. I'm convinced you must wake up at 2:30 am to be as wide-awake and strange as you are at 5 am. And I'm convinced no one makes better underwater noises than you.

This gift you have is not easily described. You mask it in many ways: as hard work, as desire, as silliness, as determination. Whatever the name, you have it and it has served you well. I cannot imagine a team without you.

Over your four years, you have created a reputation for the unexpected. Others wait with baited, chlorine breath, for your next move. They have seen you dance, sing, yell, swim like a shark, and spasm. All while leading the team through "follow the leader" warm-up. They have also seen you work hard through the toughest of practices. Your example is a beacon of light for others to see.

I have seen you grow and mature in many ways. As a leader, you have led by your actions. As a motivator, you have shown that swimming can be very difficult, but fun at the same time. As an example, you have kept swimmers focused when it was hard to see the light at the end of the tunnel. As a woman, you have proven repeatedly, that you are indeed an athlete.

Thank you for giving so much in so many ways to this swim team. It is my prayer that this gift you have serves you as well in the next four years as it has the previous four.

fleen

❖ **The Character** ❖
Elizabeth Z

My introduction to you was many years ago as a middle school student. Your unbridled enthusiasm was contagious, even if it was covered by a cheer uniform. The middle school neighbor who couldn't stop talking soon became the high school swimmer who couldn't stop talking. You have this infectious way of becoming part of something positive. Whether in school or at swim, it didn't matter. You saw the uniqueness of our swim team when you arrived and you believed in the concepts being taught. To say you were a believer is an understatement.

When you arrived you were new to the sport and new to swim. Everyone with a pool in their backyard thinks they are a swimmer. What makes you different is you have a knack for the sport. You took that natural ability and developed it into a talent. That talent carried you to CIF more than once. You practiced hard, and when you didn't feel well you still practiced hard. Your commitment and dedication to the team was a joy to watch not only this year, but every year.

You hope as a coach, that you have people who believe in you. I am grateful for your trust in me over the past four years. You have demonstrated your loyalty over and over again. Thank you for the quality of character you possess. This trait will be your guide to an unlimited future.

fleen

❖ **The Talent** ❖
Ashley H

There are not many people who are blessed with the ability to excel in a sport. You have been blessed. There are not many people who take the ability they have been given and work hard to improve it. You have done that.

In four short year's you have accomplished more than the average athlete. You have lived in the shadow of some pretty impressive swimmers. Yet you have done everything that was asked of you in order to set your own legacy. That legacy is not limited to the pool. Your academic achievements speak for themselves. Your work ethic is second to none. Your character is without question. You have seized the moment, and for that you are a better student, a better athlete, and a better person.

In four short year's you have matured in many ways. As a Freshman, you worked and watched as you did your best to carry on a tradition. It was a season of learning. That learning experience culminated at CIF in 1998 as I watched you anchor the CIF winning 200 Medley Relay. I couldn't have been happier for you at that moment. As a Sophomore, you continued to grow and enjoy the fruits of your labor by once again representing the Lions at CIF. You also saw that life, as a swimmer can sometimes be fun. As a junior, you began to realize the speed that had always been inside you. Your DVL Record in the 100 Free was clear evidence. You broke some personal barriers as an individual and as an athlete. As a senior, your leadership by example was a joy to observe. The commitment you made in every way translated directly to your success. Your time had come and you made the most of it.

As you prepare for the next four short years, it is my hope that you will continue to grow in character. That you will realize your experience is a journey, not a destination. That you will use adversity as a tool to building a better more successful you.

I am grateful to have been your coach. To have been a small stepping-stone in your life. So as you prepare to go on to college, I wish you luck. I know you will make the most of your experience. Your best is yet to come.

fleen

Chapter Two

2002

Dear Friend,

Why does a person choose to swim? Why would a person choose to swim at Cathedral City? What makes them want to swim? As a coach, I sometimes think about the reasons why they swim. One thing I have learned over the last 10 years is that the motivation is different for each person. I am OK with that. I realize that we all have many reasons why we do the things we do. What makes me most proud is that when they are asked that same question after a few years in the program, the answer is almost unanimously the same. They swim because they have fun.

Having fun. Imagine that. Getting up at 4:30 am. Getting home after 7 pm. Working until every muscle in your body hurts, while not being able to breathe. Being consistently monitored academically. Being held to the same standard whether you are a first-year or fourth-year swimmer. Does that sound like fun to you? Well if I were a new kid thinking about swimming and saw that list, I'd have some second thoughts about it.

Well, every year we get a new batch of swimmers with no idea they are about to do something they will never forget. And the returning swimmers can't wait to do it all over again. I try to let people know two things right upfront. One, swim will be nothing like they expect, and two, it will be the hardest thing they ever love. The 2002 version of Cathedral City Swim presented more challenges in one season than I've ever had. It also presented me with some of the fondest memories I've ever had.

The season would be something of an X-File. One of my favorite all time TV shows, The X-Files attempts to explain the unexplainable. Sometimes the show leaves you with no answers. I felt like Fox Mulder many times this year. I was still very passionate about what I wanted to accomplish, but sometimes I had no explanation for what was happening.

The varsity girls would be the first to experience the phenomenon. Who I thought was going to swim and who actually swam were very different from each other. The bottom line is we had many girls with little or no experience and they had little time to get it. We were able to field a full varsity squad only 5 of 12 meets. You name it and it happened to us. Sicknesses, injuries, discipline. A girl actually fell out of a tree and missed two weeks. Yet in spite of everything that happened the girls managed to go 7-5 overall and qualify 2 girls in 3 events and 2 relays for CIF. In January I would have been happy with one qualifier. Leading the way was senior captain Alexis F. The UC Irvine bound water polo player would be DVL Champion in the 100 Free and place 11th and 13th in the 50 & 100 free at CIF. She would combine with seniors Amber P, Lauren L, and freshman Mary N to qualify in the 200 & 400 free relays. Junior Natalie S would swim an amazing 100 breaststroke at DVL to qualify for that event at CIF. Mary N as well as fellow freshmen Melinda H, Jessica M, and Sheila A would all make significant contributions throughout the year.

"7" seems to be the lucky number for the boys. For the second year in a row that would be the total team. Led by seniors Adam K, Eric R, and Chris C the boys would finish 6-5-1. That is no typo. They actually tied a meet. Whoever heard of a tie in swimming? Adam K would qualify for CIF in two events for a record 4th year in a row. After working all season to try and qualify in the 50 & 100 free, he only had one automatic cut in the 100 free and three other consideration times. He ended up choosing the 200 IM and amazingly would go on to place 6th at CIF in a school record time. He would also place 11th in the 100 free. He also teamed up with Eric R, Chris C, and sophomore Tyler C to qualify in the 400 free relay.

The JV girls would surprise me as well. When the season began they were some of the least talented kids I had ever had try out. Thank goodness for the shallow end and walls close by or otherwise I probably would have had to save a few. Fortunately, early in the season, they did not have much competition and as a result, their confidence grew. It wasn't long before their ability caught up. Every meet a new girl would turn in an incredible time and "find" her event. They worked so hard and seemed to understand the things I felt were important. More than anything I could see fun in their faces. They truly liked being on the team. They would finish 11-1 and win DVL for the 6th time. A fitting finish for a wonderful bunch of girls.

What would a season be without the annual spring break trip? Santa Barbara would be the third visit for our spring break swimmers. Although the weather did not cooperate, (fog and clouds) it couldn't dampen the spirits of the kids. We had a great week of training, eating, and fun. Mix in some beach games (soccer, volleyball, and frisbee golf) outrageous team activities (see Amelia's unibrow, Danette's Alexis imitation, Chris & Alex's "dance off") and the usual surprise (whale watching on a 50 ft catamaran) and spring break 2002 was a tremendous success. The weekly winner of the team activities turned out to be the "Continuum Transformers" (I guess that's what I get for having such smart kids!?).

The 10th edition of Cathedral City Swimming proved to be the worst of times and the best of times. Wins and losses will come and go, but memories of good times had and friendships made are what is important. That is perhaps why I enjoyed this group so much. As the years go by and the kids revolve, I do not remember the wins, I remember the experiences.

I do not remember the teams, I remember the people. I do not remember the disappointments, I remember the joys. Thank you again for giving me the opportunity to serve the student-athletes at Cathedral City.

Swimmingly

❖ **The Faithful** ❖
Adam K

There are just some things you get used to having around. Like a favorite pair of shorts or that one-of-a-kind glass. Because they are familiar, you know you can rely on them. They always seem to be there when you need them. Over the last four years, many things have come and gone, but your commitment has not been one of them.

I remember seeing you as a big-eyed freshman trying to find your way. Our team has never been devoid of personality and when that personality is determined by older, energetic females, well let's just say you better be a good sport. You were always a good sport. One of your finer moments was when they dressed you up like a girl in

22

Hawaii. Your make-up artists spared no expense. Even I didn't recognize you at first.

Then came your sophomore year. You must have thought, "Why do I always end up dressed like a woman?" You were stunning if I do say so myself. I'm sure you were wondering what this whole swim team thing was all about. Was it about swimming or was it about making people look as silly as possible? Your junior year I'll never forget those famous words. "Fleen, I'm not dressing up like a girl this year!"

Through it all, you were never one to back away or say no. You have always given of yourself both in and out of the pool. When I look back at your four years, I will look back fondly at a person who worked hard and played hard. A person who understood the true meaning of competition. A person who always had a positive effect on those around him. It is those traits that will carry you to a bright future.

One of the things I absolutely enjoy about coaching is forming special relationships with people. It has been a pleasure to have been a part of your life these past four years. You will be missed as a student. You will be missed as an athlete. More importantly, you will be missed as a person.

fleen

❖ **The Decision** ❖
Alexis F

I t used to be so easy. Your freshman year it was a definite yes. Your sophomore year, although not as resounding, it was still yes. Next was your junior year. The answer was no…then yes…then no…then yes. Although I was happy with the decision, I was confused by the hesitation. Then came your senior year. I prepared myself to accept the fate of another laborious decision. I refused to listen to the hoards of others who, without hesitation, I might add, told me the answer would be no. I thought to myself, "how could the decision to swim be so difficult."

I will be the first to admit, swimming is not all that exciting. You move forward, hit a wall, reverse direction, and do it over and over and over again with only a black line to keep you company. It's hard to carry on a conversation because our communication skills underwater are somewhat limited. It's not like you ever experience the joy of making a game winning basket. Swimming is unique. That is a nice way of saying that it hurts, not some of the time, all the time. It is a mind battling, courage testing, muscle burning, character building sport. And I have news for you. This is why you swim.

I will remember three specific moments that make me most proud of you. The first is naturally at a Starbucks. We met to discuss "the junior decision." After 2 hours and way too much coffee, you decided to swim. You realized it was a means to an end. The end was water polo. That season you gave it everything you had and were such a positive contributor all year long.

The second was "the senior decision." We were sitting in front of the gym after CIF water polo practice when I asked you if you were going to swim. You said no and tried to convince yourself, I mean me, why you weren't going to swim. You then listened carefully as I offered my opinion as to why you should. When you decided to once again swim. I was so happy. Not for me, but for you. I felt your decision was the most thoughtful and mature thing I had ever seen. Even though you didn't like swimming, you knew it was necessary to achieve your dream of playing college water polo.

The third moment I will always remember will be next year when I watch you fulfill your dream of playing college water polo.

fleen

The Smile
Amber P

They say you can learn a lot about someone the first time you meet them. Four years ago I learned you could smile. That is what I remember. The smile. It is big. It is infectious. It is genuine. Like Visa, it is everywhere you want to be. Some people wear their emotions on their sleeve, you wear yours on your mouth. I have yet to see it in any other position than ends up. Every time I see you, something overcomes me, and I can't help but smile back. You should take your show on the road and charge admission. You're like a magician.

Fortunately, you are more than a smile. You are much more. You are caring. You are sincere. You are fun. You were all three when you made possibly the best "Pie in the Eye." You threw it, assisted in the clean-up, and helped Danette get it off her face. I think part of it is still stuck in her eyelash.

I have been impressed by you in so many ways. When you decided to hang up the skirt and put on a suit. When you dedicated yourself to swimming both in and out of the pool. When you did everything you could to have the best practice possible every day. When you went out of your way to make a younger athlete feel a part of the team. When you humbly enjoyed the fruits of your labor.

Your character cannot be questioned. Your desire will not be deterred. I hope you have enjoyed swimming these past two years as much as I have enjoyed watching you relish in the experience. You are exactly the kind of person who should and will succeed. Thank you for reminding me daily the reason why I enjoy coaching.

fleen

❖ **The Rollercoaster** ❖
Chris C

High School is a time where people begin to define the kind of person they will become. They experiment and try many things. They go through periods where life is about as good as it can get. Unfortunately, they also go through periods where things happen that defy explanation. It is during those times that a person's character is molded.

You have gone through your share of ups and downs in the last four years. Academically you had to struggle with the problem of being misplaced entering high school. Yet you did not complain. You made the best of it and worked to correct the problem. Later you struggled to maintain the appropriate academic standing necessary to participate in sports. Yet you managed to just make it. Still later, something happened and the light went on. Your grades were not just good, they were outstanding. Academics were no longer an issue.

Athletically, you chose to participate in two of the toughest sports on campus. To this day I don't know why you chose those sports. You did not really have a background, but you worked hard to improve yourself. It did not matter that one program was well established and the other was floundering, you were fully committed to both. You came to represent the kind of person who should and did get the most out of an athletic experience in high school. You improved tremendously, you gave of yourself fully, you were positive, and you had fun.

Outside of school you also had to deal with situations that high school kids should never have to deal with. I appreciated your honesty in always letting me know what was going on. More importantly, I respected your attitude in dealing with the situation. You were upbeat, you were genuine, and you did not let it consume you. I will remember your subtle, yet hilarious mannerisms. I will remember your "rave" ability. But mostly I will remember your character.

fleen

❖ **The Commitment** ❖
Eric R

I am constantly amazed at the type of kids that show up to swim. When they begin they always have an idea of what it will be like. When they finish they realize swim was not at all what they thought it would be like. I mean swimming is not supposed to be that fun.

When you showed up that first day, you brought with you your skeletons from the Piranhas. Your image of swimming was nurtured by long, uneventful workouts that fostered unenthusiastic results. One by one I watched as you threw bone after bone away and realized that swimming can be fun. I saw you find your place on the team. I smiled as you began to become a leader. I cheered as you became faster and faster.

I have never seen anyone in my 10 years of coaching enjoy swimming in lane one more than you. It was almost as if you couldn't wait for practice to begin so you could perform your laughable morning practice entry.

It was almost as if you discovered that swimming was not the most important thing. The most important thing was being on the

TEAM. The bus rides, the meals, the trips, the friendships. That is what is important.

I am grateful that you have had such an enjoyable experience. It has been a pleasure to watch you develop. I am glad you have given so much of yourself over the last four years.

fleen

p.s. I am also glad that nobody told you you aren't supposed to run around on deck in just shoes, socks, and a speedo.

❖ **The Tumor** ❖
Lauren L

I f you had a choice to be remembered by a word, I don't think you would choose "The Tumor." My second choice wasn't much better, "The Curse." My feeling is that the originator of "The Curse" just rotated "The Tumor" throughout your body. How else could you explain the barrage of calamities that have attacked you in only three years of swimming? I do not believe it is a coincidence that your mother is a nurse. You need all the help you can get.

The Tumor began in your brain as a freshman when, against my advice, you decided to become a cheerleader. The only consolation was that the tumor was small and was removed after one short year. From that point on the tumor moved fast and furious. To a finger, then a toe, then a shoulder, then the stomach, an eyelash. NO body part was safe. In your throat, the tumor mutated. Finally, after I threatened to remove them, your tonsils were taken out and even then you were not immune from "The Tumor." One step forward, seven steps back, pretty much sums it up.

Amid everything, there was one shining star. You always bounced back. As frustrated as you would become, you never let it consume you. I saw early in you a talent for the sport. It seemed so natural. I had to smile every time you would turn in an amazing time without the training necessary to produce it. "How could she do that?" I would ask myself. The tumor must be in remission I would conclude.

You have so much potential. Not only as an athlete, but also as a student and a person. You have demonstrated time and again that you are more than ready for what life throws at you. I have no doubt that as you move on in life, you will rise above.

fleen

Chapter Three

2003

Dear Friend,

Imagine what it is like to have three months of your life become a total blur. Some people can only stare at the clock each day hoping time will somehow go by faster than it did the day before. Imagine remembering what it was like to celebrate Valentine's Day like it was yesterday. Only it wasn't yesterday, it was three months ago. Instead of my thoughts being on our first meet or our spring break trip, my thoughts are on the end of school and my summer plans. Three months to most feels like an eternity. For me, it felt like three hours. The only difference was what 50 high school student-athletes and I were able to experience. Victories, defeats, joys, disappointments, failures, and successes. Imagine experiencing all that almost daily for three months. Only then can you begin to understand why I consider it a privilege to coach swimming at Cathedral City High School.

This year as usual we were not blessed with an abundance of "club kids" as they are known. We didn't have any. What we did have was an abundance of kids who wanted to work, get better, and most importantly, enjoy what they were about to begin doing for the next three months. It all begins in February with what we jokingly call tryouts. Jokingly because we don't and have never cut anyone. Kids from other sports on campus who are unfamiliar with our program always want to know if they've "made it." With a smile, I tell them the only way they wouldn't "make it" is if they didn't come back tomorrow. As usual, they kept coming back.

The Girls Varsity team would go 6-6 in duals while losing three very close meets along the way. Their success would become a team effort. Many would stand out each meet and make the difference. Seniors Christy G and Natalie S, juniors Jillian F and Jessica D, and sophomores Mary N, Melinda H, and Michelle L would all contribute. Even freshman Alyssa A would play a role in the team's success. With limited experience, they battled meet after meet and improved. A move from Division III to Division II would mean they would have to be even faster to qualify anyone for CIF. That is a tall task for an inexperienced team. Happily, through their efforts, they would qualify 2 relays (200 & 400 free) and Jillian F would qualify in the 50 & 100 free. I was pleased they could enjoy the fruits of their labor.

The Varsity Boys team would be even more inexperienced than the girls. They would return only 1 ½ people. Sophomore Alex U would be the 1, and junior Cory A would be the half. Half because Cory would break his arm snowboarding the week before swim was to begin. He didn't let that slow him down. He would wear a rubber-suctioning sleeve to keep his hand to armpit cast dry. On a team that spares no expense for anyone, Cory would become affectionately known as "Gumby." The team would manage to win four meets and discover some talented swimmers in sophomore Daniel C and freshman Austin K.

The JV Girls team is always a joy to watch develop. This year would be no different. Seeing 25 new kids go through the struggles of their development is nothing compared to the smiles on their faces when they see themselves improve. Six would see themselves swimming Varsity at some point during the season.

They were a pretty talented group that would go 10-2 overall and 6-1 in DVL. I don't think I've ever had so many voluntarily come to morning practice. They would come to realize that the only limitation to how quickly they improved would be themself.

Spring break has a whole different meaning for swimmers on our campus. This year it meant Hawaii. What a trip! Incredible fun and non-stop action. When I do room checks at night and everyone is not only in their rooms, but already asleep, I know I've done my job. It would be a trip they won't soon forget. Snorkeling with sea turtles, visiting Pearl Harbor, jumping off rocks on the North Shore with "local boys," experiencing a sunset Luau, walking along the crater of a volcano. It was hard to choose a best moment.

So here we are in June and all I can think about is next year. How we can become a better swim team. My hope is that many will work hard between now and then to turn their inexperience into experience. As I know all too well, time has a way of flying by when you are having fun.

Thank you again for supporting us and allowing me to provide a framework that makes kids successful.

Swimmingly

❖ **The Poster Child** ❖
Chelsea R

Why does someone subject themselves to endless practices, early mornings, constant accountability, and enduring discomfort? I honestly ask myself that very question every year. The kids I get don't usually have a background in swim or water polo. Why would someone in their right mind choose a sport they knew little about and had no experience with? I've discovered the answer lies in the question. They must not be in their right mind.

You have become the poster child for the aquatic athlete at Cathedral City. You did not possess the things that a coach looks for naturally, i.e. experience and skill, but you worked hard and obtained them. You did not have great knowledge of either sport, but you know more now than most people will forget. You did not know what it meant to be on a team, now you will never forget.

You have become what every coach dreams of having. An athlete who is committed, works hard, has fun, and makes sure those around her are trying their best to do the same. I never heard you complain, I never saw you give anything less than your best, and I never saw you elevate yourself at the expense of someone else. You saw yourself rise to an All-League position and you saw yourself fall from a large tree position. Through it all, you have epitomized the aquatic student/athlete at Cathedral City.

You have become a woman of true integrity who has not only prepared a bright path for the future but has also left a legacy that won't soon be forgotten.

fleen

❖ The Language ❖
Christy G

Languages are what allow us to communicate. They enable us to share a mood, a feeling, an emotion. You and I, for some reason, have seemed to develop our own style of communicating over the years. It is usually only understood by us, and sometimes we don't even understand. We would make short comments that had no relation. We would watch as those around us would try to understand what it was we were talking about. The more intently they listened the more bizarre and random our comments would become. Eventually, they would turn away thinking there was something internally wrong with us. Sometimes it was just sounds. The infamous "guusshh." Others could only pretend to comprehend. It is not often that I make that "connection" with someone. I tend to not only think outside the box; oftentimes I am nowhere near the box. That is where I found you. That unspoken bond is one of the first things I noticed about you.

I was happy you swam as a freshman then sad when you didn't as a sophomore. Happily, these past two years have been a joy for both of us. You have this ability to make others, including myself, forget about the immediate uneasiness and focus on the immediate absurd. A look, a sound, a dance, an expression is usually all it would take. I have appreciated your ability to keep people in check using this skill. You grew to know the difference between comedic focus and comic relief. I know many times it must not have been as easy as it looked, in light of the health issues facing your mother.

Thank you for being yourself and coming to understand me as I am. I look forward to the future when I will see you and nothing will be understood by anyone around us... except you and me.

fleen

❖ **The Athlete Mentality** ❖
Danette D

The athlete mentality is a hard thing to understand. There is no definition and I have heard no one describe it to me so that I understood. I have no idea what a game face is either, but I've heard many people talk about the need to put one on. Sports has a way of putting you in the position of both student and teacher. That is where you and I are similar. It is also where you and I are different.

When you began your eventful sports career, you probably knew as much about swimming as I did when I began. You knew we had a team and you knew you could be a part of it. Like a newborn child, you soaked up information like a sponge. It was at those moments that you became the student. It didn't seem to matter that you knew nothing before you began. You simply gave it your best and let the chips fall where they may. Happily for you, they seemed to have fallen into place rather nicely.

Your athlete mentality told you that to improve you had to be committed. Being committed is easier when you enjoy what you are doing. That was always evident with you. It appeared you appreciated the journey as much as you did the destination. The highs were never too high and the lows were never too low. That perspective is unique. It was a perspective that was not lost to me. I would see you not take yourself or the situation too seriously. It was hard at times for me to understand your athlete mentality, while at other times it was a refreshingly clear outlook on an otherwise difficult circumstance. It was at those moments that you became the teacher. Those around you noticed and so did I.

I have do not doubt that the lessons you learned and the lessons you taught will serve you well as you leave this place. As the saying goes, "you are never too old to learn," it should also say "you are never too young to teach."

fleen

❖ **The Medicated** ❖
Natalie S

Time is that uncontrollable part of our life. We can't slow it down or speed it up. As much as we hate to admit it, we are at its mercy. So it goes with you. You have been at the mercy of time for quite a while now. When you were sick or injured it couldn't go by fast enough. When you felt great it never seemed to last long enough. I think you are the only athlete I've ever had who could have seasons within a season. Every year had to feel more like two or three.

You would ride the physical and emotional roller coaster every single year. When it came to you, I never took anything for granted. I had to treat every day like it was your last healthy day. You must be the reason they invented health insurance. Some of the medications you took I've never heard, and I know about that stuff.

The funny thing is I don't think I've ever had anyone experience more out of swim than you. Describing your 4 years is like being the pastor of a wedding ceremony: "for richer for poorer, in sickness and in health, till death do us part." That pretty much sums up your high school experience. You have experienced the richness when you qualified for CIF on your last attempt of the year, then the poorness as you became sick the very next day. When you were trained and healthy you were a joy to watch swim. Your determination was as easy to see as the sun itself. Your breaststroke appeared incredibly strong, yet gracefully effortless.

In the midst of all your trials and tribulations, the one constant has been your willingness to contribute to the success of the team in any way possible. As frustrated as you might have been, you never lost sight of the goal. Your perseverance did not go unnoticed. Five years from now when I'm telling kids stories about hanging in there, they will know the name Natalie S.

fleen

❖ The Student ❖
Sheri C

A blur. That is what these past 4 years have been. I remember a very green freshman who didn't say much, but worked hard to make a place for herself. I remember a sophomore who couldn't wait to do it all over again. I remember a junior who finally came out of her shell and continued to enjoy swim and all that it involved. I remember a senior who was so excited she was finally going to Hawaii. I'm sure the fact that you threatened me with bodily harm if we didn't, had something to do with it.

One of the things I am most proud of as a coach is people who come in with no expectation and leave the same way. They simply try their best every day, they give to the betterment of the team, and they never expect anything in return. It is those people who truly get the most out of swim. You have been that person. When you look back on your high school experience you will remember the good times with friends, the spring break trips, the bus rides, and the cheering. Most importantly you will remember the togetherness.

You have done your best these past 4 years to carry on the traditions that have been passed on to you. There is a level of maturity that develops when you grow through the program. It teaches people selflessness. It teaches people humility. It teaches people sportsmanship. It teaches people the true meaning of pride. In that regard, you have been a top student. You have been a student who will no doubt carry with you the lessons you learned and the lessons you taught for the rest of your life.

fleen

Chapter Four

2004

Dear Friend,

They say there are two kinds of people. Those who love to wake up early for swim practice and those who hate people who love to wake up early for swim practice. OK, maybe the saying doesn't quite go like that. What can you expect, I'm a swim coach. The point is they have to wake up early for swim practice. Although they may not like to wake up early for swim practice, they still do. Would you wake up early? Some people set their alarm to the minute to get the most available sleep possible, only to finally get up and realize they think they need more. So they still feel tired and they also haven't accomplished much yet. I don't know one swimmer who ever regretted waking up early for swim practice when, at the end of the season, they just swam the race of their life in a time they never thought was possible. How did they do it? I know, they worked for it.

I am always pleasantly surprised by the results I get from my athletes. Every year I get a new batch of athletes who have no idea what they are about to accomplish during the next three months. In that time they will develop lasting friendships, work harder than they ever have before... and enjoy it. They will travel across America. They will see their body metamorphosis into the body of an athlete. They will cry tears of joy. Finally, they will not know what to do with themselves when that fateful day comes when they don't have to go to practice anymore. The 2004 version of Cathedral City Swim experienced all of the above.

This team was not much different than my 2nd team when they began. It was about the same size and about the same talent level. A friend once called my 2nd team "talently challenged." I had to agree with them...at the beginning of the season, but certainly not at the end. This year's team was like that. They improved more than almost any team I have ever had.

Inexperienced teams usually have trouble paying attention to detail. In swimming, detail is extremely important. That would quickly become a recurring theme. The Varsity Girls team would have a record of 6-5-1. That looks more like a hockey record than a swim record. You aren't supposed to tie after 11 events, 30 swims, and 170 points. We did. You aren't supposed to lose another meet by two points. We did. You aren't supposed to drop seven seconds in one day and just miss a CIF cut. We did. The Varsity Boys team would only swim six boys each meet. You aren't supposed to win meets with only six boys. We did. Those types of teams aren't supposed to qualify kids for CIF. We did. The JV Girls team would change weekly as many found themselves on varsity for whatever reason. That would leave a mismatch of JV girls swimming each week. Those teams aren't supposed to experience much success. They did. They actually experienced it eight times.

Like my athletes, I remember many things about the season that had nothing to do with swimming. I remember watching kids laughing as we hogtied five kids together who had birthdays during the season and then smothered their faces with birthday cake. I remember them being so excited when they got on the plane to go to Washington D.C. for spring break, then see most fall asleep because they hadn't slept much the night before in anticipation of the trip. I remember Vivian Z using some pretty cheesy pick-up lines on the "swim boys" from the University of Maryland. I remember David F wearing Cristina M's skirt, and actually looking better in it than she did!? I remember Isai V shaving his head on "shave nite" and look like Mr. T at one point. I remember Mary N finally making a CIF cut in the 100 free at DVL, the slowest of six DVL girls who qualified, then swim faster than any of them at CIF. I remember watching Alex U go from this novice swimmer as a freshman to a School Record holder and CIF qualifier this year. I remember parents and coaches of opposing teams congratulating me on a meet with us and immediately ask when we can swim them again next year. All because they enjoyed swimming against us so much...and they lost the meet!

What do you remember about the last three months? I can only hope your last three months were as enjoyable as mine. Thank you again for making the program these kids are able to be a part of possible. Your generosity does not go unnoticed.

Swimmingly

❖ **The Nickname** ❖
Cory A

I can't believe I am at this point. When I sat down to write this letter I couldn't believe this moment had finally come. It was both difficult and easy to write. Easy because I have so many fond memories of your time in the program and difficult because I have so many fond memories of your time in the program. My first swim kids felt like they had been around for so long because we had experienced so much together. That is how it feels with you as if you've been a part of the program for at least 7 years. Are you really graduating?

I was glad football didn't quite work out for you. Glad you discovered swimming was the next logical sport to try. You were the perfect freshman. You had fun, worked hard, and took your abuse like a man. No one in the history of swimming has had more nicknames than you. Lifeguard, 911, Gumby, Role Cole & Baywatch are but a few. Whether we had many boys or just a few, you always seemed to be the one the girls liked to make their next, and continuing victim. We could have been a three-person team and you would still have been the odd one out. For some reason, that scenario appeared to be a recurring theme throughout your sophomore… and junior…and as fate would have it, your senior year as well. Lucky you!

I was so impressed by your commitment, your respect for others, your willingness to work hard, and your desire to be a part of the solution. When you broke your arm one week before swim began your junior year, I honestly didn't expect to see you until your cast came off in April. I thought I might see you at team meals, but certainly not at practice. Imagine my surprise when, on your own, you had researched a rubber suctioning sleeve to put over your cast, bought it, and showed up for one of the first practices. Then you showed up for morning practice as well. All you could do was kick, and you hate kicking! That was when all of us, athletes and coaches, started to question your sanity. I honestly don't know if any athlete I've ever had would go to such extremes to be a part of something. It was at that moment that I realized you were not the average high school student/athlete. You represented more, much more.

Thank you for being such an example for me and to the other athletes. Your true character, like your nicknames, will be hard to replace.

Fleen

❖ The Dessert ❖
Gaby S

Where do I begin? How do I convey respect? How do I demonstrate appreciation? For three years you have been a part of something I don't think either one of us thought you would be a part of. Maybe that is why you kept coming back. We aren't your average athletic team. We aren't driven by the ultimate athletic accomplishment. I think we are, among other things, driven by character accomplishment. I think that might be one of the reasons you kept coming back, because you have been blessed with tremendous character.

You have been a beacon for "Lion Pride." I enjoyed watching you enjoy yourself and your teammates. I think it is because you are the ultimate teammate. You quickly learned what our program was about and you represented that belief consistently. I gain no greater joy than watching someone like you watch, reach, struggle, and succeed. Because I know that other people are seeing the same thing. They see your enthusiasm. They see your determination. They see you hurt and they see you smile. A big, big smile with an equally big laugh. I will miss them both.

In Washington D.C. this spring, Lyndee H (Class of '97) made the comment. "They're girls Fleen, you don't understand, you'll never understand." While I acknowledge her keen insight (she is, after all, a girl) I am not sure she is entirely correct. I present you as exhibit A. You are like one of my favorite desserts, apple pie…a la mode of course. It may not look the same from top to bottom, but it is sweet all the way through. As I discovered one layer after another, I learned that all of them were wonderfully fresh. At times I believe that frustrated you, the fact that I knew you so well. Your strengths as well as your weaknesses. You loved to play "complicated," but both of us knew you were relatively easy to know, love, and appreciate. You knew right from wrong, just like I did, but you would test me anyway secretly hoping the answer might be different while all the time knowing it wouldn't.

I have no doubt you will always remember your time here. I will always remember your time here as well. I also do not doubt that your true character will deliver you to a place neither one of us could dream of or imagine.

fleen

❖ **The Learner** ❖
Lindsay B

They say the true test of a person is what they do when no one is watching. Some say it is how they respond to adversity. I say it is what Lindsay B has shown over the last three years.

As a freshman, you wanted to swim, but came out too late to join the team. At the time you were very quiet and shy. I distinctly remember the look of sincere disappointment on your face. To your credit, you came back as a sophomore with tremendous enthusiasm. You were probably the first person to come see me about fundraising. With a vengeance, you raised the money and had a great experience that year in Santa Barbara. I could see the character in you exploding.

With each practice and each year you would become more and more animated, the team and its members would become more and more important to you. You would evolve from that quiet follower to the energetic instigator. I was shocked and extremely proud when on a quiet bus, you would begin a cheer. And although your voice would crack a few times you were never too embarrassed to finish the cheer.

It was times like these that I knew you understood what swimming at Cathedral City was all about. It's about fun. You always knew the traditions we had and how to make them fun for yourself as well as others. It's about growth, not only as a person, but also as an athlete. You were not overly talented, but you improved more in one year than some do in four. You no doubt made the most of your talents. It's about creating lasting friendships. The minute you see a former swimmer, you will feel that bond immediately no matter how much time has elapsed. It's about doing more than just showing up for practice.

I am grateful and thankful that for the last three years you have done more than just show up. You have learned the true meaning of Cathedral City Swimming.

fleen

❧ **The Swimmer?**
Vivian E

I f there is one thing I have learned over the years, it's that I am no closer to understanding why people choose to swim. Case in point, Vivian E. At first, I thought it was because your friends joined, then they quit the next year and you still swam. Then I thought it was because you enjoyed the nature of the sport, swimming back and forth, and back …and forth. Training your body to do things humanly impossible. I quickly learned that wasn't it either. Then I thought it was because you enjoyed my coaching so much. I think we both know that wasn't the reason.

Then I had a revelation. You joined swim because you like to dance! I don't know why I hadn't seen it before. It was so obvious. Every year, while I was editing clips for the swim video, I seemed to have more clips of you dancing than I had of you swimming. It became too clear to me. Waking up for morning practice was just your way of stretching out those dance muscles from swim practice the night before. During study hall, when I was naïve enough to think you were actually studying, you were reading about the latest dance move. I must say your dedication has paid off. No one does the "hoochie pop" better than you. I mean that move is pretty much like doing freestyle on solid ground.

While I may not completely understand the inner workings of your mind, I do appreciate your dedication to the team. I watched and admired from a distance how you chose a path that was different than that of many of your friends. You believed school was important, and you continued to commit yourself to the AVID program. You made me proud when you spoke of your responsibilities at the city council meeting. You appeared so natural in that setting and in your interactions with the adults who were present.

I hope you look back at your time in swim as something that prepared you for your future in some small way. A place that let you have fun. A place that allowed you to meet different people. More importantly, a place that gave you a stage for your dance moves.

fleen

Chapter Five

2005

Dear Friend

A friendly smile, a cheer of joy, the look of accomplish filled disbelief, uncontrollable laughter, the anguish of knowing you gave everything you had, tears of happiness.

This is my office.

It is where I go to work each morning and afternoon. It is the place where time stands still and the clock is both important and irrelevant. It is important because it is my most valuable asset. It is irrelevant because it does not tell me when my job is done. It does not have control over me. I have control over it.

This is my office.

I have a computer that can store files of what I have done. I have a memory that can store more. I can type words, but they cannot express the true feeling behind them. My computer only does what I command it to do. The student/athletes entrusted to me give me more than I could ever expect or imagine.

This is my office.

I wake up each day knowing that I will always be surprised. I take nothing for granted because I do not work with tools; I work with minds, bodies, and souls. For me, the destination is not the reward I seek. For me, the path I create to that destination is the single most important reason I go to my office every day.

This is my office. I am a coach.

As I look back on another year of teaching kids determination, work ethic, goal setting, desire, integrity through sportsmanship, and pride, I am constantly reminded how lucky I am to be in this position. Not many jobs give you the chance to experience life from a different angle every day. I guess that is why I love coaching at Cathedral City so much. In the best of times and worst of times, we are still not like any other high school I have seen. I am proud of that.

This year was not much different than years past. We still worked hard, we still had more fun than most teams will ever have, we still created memories and friendships the kids will never forget, we still won more meets than we lost, and we still had champions. I am proud that we gave new kids the opportunity to believe in their own abilities both academically and athletically.

Freshmen Kyle K, Michael P, and Jay F all saw swim from a perspective they did not anticipate when the season began. I think all of their expectations were surpassed. I am proud that when the four boys, who made up the entire team, look back on the season their first thoughts won't be of wins and losses, but good times had and improvements made.

Almost every girl on the team had the opportunity to swim Varsity at some point during the season. I have to remind my athletes how much ability they have hidden in themselves they don't even know about. This was never more evident than with Brittany Z. To say she came from humble beginnings would be an understatement. Yet there she was swimming Varsity on more than a few occasions. Danielle G, Cristina M, and Andrianna M all fought through unique adversities unrelated to swim, yet still found ways to remain focused and have successful seasons.

Thank you again for caring enough to support a program that does more than just teach kids how to swim.

Swimmingly

❖ The Situation ❖
Crystal C

Life is ultimately about situations. We face them each year, each day, each minute, and each second. It is what we do with those situations that determine who we are. When you chose to swim, I did not know you well. Since that day I have come to know you better than you think. I have learned you are conscientious, I have learned you are motivated, I have learned you are determined, and I have learned you are a woman of character.

Quiet people are sometimes hard to reach, hard to understand. I never felt this way about you. Even though you never put yourself in the center of attention, I sensed it never bothered you. Just being yourself and enjoying the moments as they have come these past few years was enough. As a coach, I feel I have a responsibility to make sure every person maximizes their talent and has as much fun as humanly possible. I am so happy for you because I believe you have.

I always felt you enjoyed swimming. This year it was obvious you enjoyed swimming more than I thought. You embody the essence of high school sports. Learning, growing, adapting and enjoying. You have personified everything I feel is important, and because of that you have gained the most.

I will not worry about you in the future. I will not be surprised when you tell me you have reached your goals. Just as I have ever since you began swimming, I will smile and tell you "good job."

fleen

❖ The Logic ❖
Jazmin M

People say the funniest things sometimes. Two people will look at a situation and view it from two completely different perspectives. Then there is you. How you come up with some of your rationale is beyond me. I thoroughly enjoyed how you would explain a given situation. Asking for clarification was useless, but I would do it anyway, just for fun. So many times I wanted to write down your words and put them in a book called "Jazisms."

Perhaps that is why you joined swim. I say perhaps because I don't think I'll ever really know. What I do know is your perspective of swim was refreshing. You may not have understood why we did the things we did, but you would do them anyway. You always appeared to ponder my underlying principle. When I saw your wheels spinning I would get excited because I knew, hiding somewhere, was a thought process I would never expect.

Maybe that is why you are such a good writer. You can either take the main road or the road less traveled. Your path has always been unique, yet always lined with sincere thought. You are kind and caring. You are content and cheerful. I can't remember you without a smile. Even in the midst of your broken ankle, a smile was never far from your face. I realize now it could have been the drugs, but I know it was more than that. Thank you for bringing your distinct personality to the team. I will miss our times in school and at practice. Rest assured, stories will be told to future swimmers about Jazmin M. Many will probably not understand why I told it, but I'll enjoy telling them anyway.

fleen

❖ **The Soul** ❖
Mary N

How do you prepare for the inevitable? How can time go by so fast? How do you put sincere thanks on paper? How do you describe the appropriate level of appreciation? When it is time to move on, how do you say goodbye?

When you began four years ago I saw something in you that I knew was special. It wasn't just your athletic ability or your academic readiness. It was your soul. It was difficult to see at first, but I knew it was unique. As the years have passed it has been such a pleasure for me to watch your soul grow. To watch it mature. To watch it shine.

I have so many fond memories of you. Some are obvious. NO ONE dances or will ever dance like you. On a pole, in a subway, on a car or in a bus, it didn't matter... you have skills. Strangely enough, you are not the only swimmer to rip a hole in her pants while wearing them. I don't think anyone has ever been so happy to finally be "pied in the eye."

Other memories have been reserved for the eyes of a few. The times you cared for your teammates. The pain on your face after giving your all in practice. The faded morning practice smile. The selfless act of placing others before yourself. Putting your priorities before high school drama.

For four years you have been the epitome of a Cathedral City swimmer. You worked hard and were committed each day both academically and athletically. You quickly understood the traditions and why they are so important. You had more fun with people you probably would never have met. You laughed and cried at the right times and you never questioned why. Most importantly, you will leave here with more memories than others will have in their lifetime.

Thank you for having faith in me. Thank you for allowing me to know a part of your soul.

fleen

❖ **The Bank** ❖
Melinda H

I had a coach once who loved to use the term "Take it to the bank." Actually, he had many expressions, most of which he used to motivate us and most of which I did not understand. This is baseball, I thought, why is this guy talking about economics? When I would pitch and we needed to get an important out, he would yell at me, "Take it to the bank!" Finally, I asked him why he always said that. He said it was because he was not worried about the situation and he had faith in me that I would do what was necessary.

It is now 2005 and life has come full circle, only now I am the coach and you are me. Although I have not used that term on you, it is how I feel about your commitment to the program. In the last four years, you have never wavered in your loyalty to me, your teammates, or yourself. High school is a difficult time and many demands are placed on kids. I am proud that you have not only weathered the storm, many times you have risen above. You have accepted the challenge and done what was necessary.

I have appreciated that you have not needed to be told what is expected. You have always taken it upon yourself to do what was necessary. Whether it was working hard in practice, encouraging teammates, staying up late to finish your homework, organizing something for the team, or fundraising for you and your dad for the last four years, you have accepted the challenge and done what was necessary.

I am so thankful that kids have seen your example. I am so grateful that you have demonstrated to me your dedication to ideals I feel are important in high school sports. I am so happy that you have given yourself and your family the best start possible to the next four years by "Taking it to the bank" these past four years.

Thank you, for accepting the challenge and doing what was necessary.

fleen

Chapter Six

2006

Dear Friend,

Even though I rarely see movies, I consider myself a fan. A few years ago there was a movie starring Bill Murray called <u>Groundhog Day.</u> The movie had a simple premise. Bill Murray discovered he could relive each day as if it had never happened before. He experienced the same situations each day and the only thing that was different was his response. It led to some hilarious moments complete with the usual love interest.

It got me thinking. My life each day as a coach is similar to the movie only I am not Bill Murray; I am everything that remained constant in his life each day. Throughout my years of coaching, I have developed a framework. That framework is what I believe will make my athletes better students, swimmers, and ultimately better people.

The Bill Murray of the movie is every athlete that decides they want to be a swimmer at Cathedral City. They all come from different backgrounds, different motivations, and different abilities. While my framework remains constant, they have the chance to learn more than just how to be a swimmer.

The 2006 version of Cathedral City Swim was rewarding in many ways. Academically we maintained our usual high standards. Athletically we had tremendous team success and found many new athletes with incredible ability. We represented our school well and quickly learned the meaning of 'Lions Pride.'

The JV Girls are probably my favorite team to watch. Like a newborn child, they would experience something new every meet. They relive their new found successes until the next one comes. Each week they learn something new and exciting that stays with them throughout the season. This year's group was truly unique in this way. Once they learned to trust their coaches, they saw themselves improve by leaps and bounds, both in the classroom and in the pool.

Jessica R, Tiffany S, and Jackie W all made continuous and amazing discoveries about their abilities. Without ever fielding a full team of 12 girls, they went relatively unchallenged on their way to an undefeated season. As always, I was more pleased with their development and buying into the team framework than I was about them going 12-0.

The Varsity Girls team came to understand the true meaning of team. Even though many believe swimming is an individual sport, no program makes it more of a team sport than we do. With practically a new line up each week, with no club swimmers, with only one qualifying for CIF, and with almost half having little or no swimming background, the girls would epitomize the meaning of 'team' on their way to 10 wins and 2 losses. More than a few times we swam teams with multiple CIF level swimmers and even though we didn't win many battles, we managed to win a lot of wars.

A small core of returning swimmers including Vivian Z, Madisyn B, and Andrianna M, mixed with a hardworking group of new swimmers like Rachel F, Jenny R, Ashley R, BreeAnna G, and Amber H, this team would surprise many of their opponents with their unique depth of quality. This was never more evident than in our last dual meet against rival PalmSprings. We lost to Pam Springs the previous year by 62 points. They returned swimmers with individual and relay CIF qualifying times. In the end we would swim our hearts out and win by 20. I was so proud of them.

The Varsity Boys team would face its evil nemesis once more; numbers. We have always been able to produce quality swimmers, what we can't produce is the boy. With pretty much six boys, and sometimes just four, the boys would actually win six meets. In two of the meets, we won every single event and lost the meet. While depth was a strength for the girls, it was a glaring weakness for the boys.

Quality, however, was not a problem. Leading the way were two DVL Champions and two CIF qualifiers. Senior Austin K was the DVL Champion in the 100 Back. He also qualified for CIF in that event. Sophomore Jay F repeated as DVL Champion in the 100 Breast and qualified in that event as well as the 500 Free for CIF. Joining Austin K and Jay F in qualifying the 200 Medley and 400 Free relays were sophomore Kyle K (3rd in the 50 Free and 2nd in the 100 Back at DVL) and freshman Brandon F (3rd 200 IM and 7th 100 Fly at DVL). It was quite a year for the boys.

The annual spring break trip went without a hitch. Unlike last year when one of the girls broke her ankle at the beach in Santa Barbara, this year no one was hurt and everyone had a great time. The usual surprise came on the first day. Instead of going to the hotel in San Diego first, we went directly to a Padres game. Most were not really baseball fans, even if their coach played in college. Still, they had a fantastic time. The weather was awesome, the training was high quality, and the team activities were what made the week extremely memorable. The Flamboyant Thespians won the weekly competitions in spectacular fashion. Laughing all the way to victory. While these training weeks are truly very fun, they are ultimately a valuable learning tool to teach kids about camaraderie, sacrifice, teamwork, and encouragement. Cathedral City Swim remains unique in being the only team that I know who annually takes their swimmers somewhere in the country for a training week.

I am extremely grateful that you have chosen to support my program. I am sure you have many choices when you are asked to support local fundraising efforts. I want to assure you that the support you give makes an incredible difference. It makes it possible for me to continue to create my framework of inclusion each and every year, for kids to be lifted from any financial burdens, and for kids to leave the program with many positive memories. Thank you.

Swimmingly

❖ **The Gift** ❖
Austin K

Without a doubt, Christmas is one of my favorite times of the year. It is a time of family, food, and gifts. Over the years the reason I enjoy it so much has changed. As an adult, I've learned the gift is what the day represents and the chance to spend time with my family. As an adolescent, I learned there is often more joy in giving than in receiving. As a child, it was always about the gifts. First, it was the exhausting journey of anticipation before the gift, then finally the volcanic elation after the grand opening.

It is not often that a swimmer reminds me of Christmas. After all, we live in an oven with palm trees, and spring is not winter. Yet you gave both of us a gift…twice. The gift was you.

When I opened you for the first time as a freshman, you were family before you knew you were family; swim family that is. Your older brother came beautifully wrapped as a freshman complete with a bow. You, on the other hand, arrived as a long thin angel hair pasta box wrapped in a combination of foil and wet toilet paper. You hadn't swum before, you didn't know how to train, and unless you were wet, the wind would blow you away.

To my surprise, you quickly endeared yourself to your teammates. It became abundantly clear you were no stranger to food. Where it went after it went inside you remained a mystery. Finally, you were added to the list of "Swim Freaks". Cathedral City Swim defines a freak as anyone whose fastest stroke is something other than freestyle.

Then for some reason, you wrapped yourself up again.

When I opened you up for the second time as a senior, you reminded me why I enjoy my swim family so much. You are spontaneously hilarious to a fault; you consume amazing amounts of food unchallenged, and your athletic ability can only be described as God given. It is my hope that as you grow older, you will not be tempted to wrap yourself up again to be opened at some later date. Let others see and enjoy the true gift that is you. More importantly, I hope you learn to see the gift in yourself.

fleen

❖ **The Hidden Treasure** ❖
Brianna F

Hurry up. Slow down. Hurry up. Slow down. This is unfortunately the life that many of us observe each day. We see it when we drive, when we shop, and when we eat. It's like the man with the TV remote. He's not really interested in what's on; he's interested in what else is on. People are coming and going so fast that many times opportunities may be missed or treasures may not be discovered.

I wish I could say that a senior joining swim for the first time is unusual, but it is not. It happens much more than I'd like to admit. I wish I could also say that most of these first time seniors are not very gifted, but unfortunately, they are. I say unfortunately because many times these people have never discovered their own hidden treasure.

When they do, the season and the experience are over.

You, Brianna, are a hidden treasure. You are a hidden treasure for many reasons. I'm not sure you saw it in softball, maybe not even water polo, but in swim it was there for you and everyone else to see. You worked, you learned, you committed, you sacrificed, and then you improved. In a short amount of time, you became an incredible swimmer.

In addition, you understood and came to quickly contribute to, our unique sense of team. Probably without realizing it, you represented to others the distinctive attributes we feel are important to our team; dedication, desire, sportsmanship, humility, and humor.

I'll never forget your remarkable ability to tan nicely everywhere on your body, except your face. I'll never forget the joy on your face when you swam your best time in your last race, and I'll never forget the hidden treasures we both discovered about you throughout the season.

Rest assured that when we see each other in the future, I will hug you first and sock you second. I will hug you for allowing me the pleasure of coaching you to such amazing heights in just one season, and then I will sock you for the very same reason.

fleen

❖ **The Choice** ❖
Britney Z

Everyday we are faced with choices that will shape our day, month, year, and ultimately our life. It often feels that as a high school student those choices are unfairly magnified. It is sometimes the easiest of choices that have the biggest impact.

You were faced with such a decision once. "Should I swim?", "Should I play polo?" I'm sure that at the moment you had to make those decisions, the choice was easy. You had just come from the first water polo practice of your life. When you had to decide whether to continue, I'm sure the choice was easy. You would have rather branded your forehead with a cattle prod reading "I'm a dork" rather than go back a second day. To say the least, it was difficult for you. At the time, polo was an unknown for you and in the end, the choice was easy and obvious.

A few years later you were faced with another choice, to decide whether to try again, only this time the situation was not unknown and the choice was more complex. "Would the risk exceed the reward?" "Would I enjoy the sport enough to try something that did not come naturally the first time?"

It is choices like these that shape us, that define us, that show us who we are. Should I float downstream or should I take the road less traveled? Many people often follow a path chosen by circumstance. It is called the path of least resistance. It is rarely difficult and is equally less rewarding.

In the few years you have been a part of my program, I have learned you are not the type of person to choose such a path for yourself. You haven't chosen it academically and you haven't chosen it athletically.

When it was difficult, you smiled and tried again. When you were tired, you focused and pushed harder. When you were offered the choice, you did not compromise. It is because you understand this concept of risk versus reward that makes me most proud to have coached you.

fleen

❖ **The Diamond** ❖
Darlene P

There are many reasons why I continue to enjoy coaching so much. I receive so many intangible rewards at the end of each season that I don't need to look at wins and losses to determine how successful we are as a team or me as a coach. One of the things I do look for are diamonds.

Diamonds are precious, and apparently a girl's best friend. Scientifically, they are formed from carbon atoms treated under pressure and temperature deep in the earth's core. Swimmingly, I believe diamonds are formed from committed, sincere people who strive to learn and do their absolute best. Darlene P, you are a diamond.

When I first met you it was clear that you were a diamond. I don't exactly remember why you chose to swim. All I remember is that you were a diamond. You had a glow that was immediately recognized by everyone.

You quickly came to represent what diamonds of Cathedral City Swim have always been about. You are about character, sacrifice, academics, baggy eyes, and a distinct aroma. You developed the usual abnormal love for bagels with cream cheese and you are one of the best belly dancing, front seat D.J.'s on swim trips, ever! You even accepted the challenges of your "swimmer buddy" and quickly shaped her into your own little diamond

There are many types of diamonds. You most resemble a "Glassy diamond." These kinds of diamonds come out clean from the mines and do not require polishing. Like you, these diamonds are very rare.

As I feel much too often, having coached you for only two seasons, I will not get to see the full unveiling of such a precious stone.

Each time I see you from now on I will smile and think about the time, energy, and resources that have gone into discovering the diamond that is you.

fleen

❖ **The Motivation** ❖
Isai V

Many times when kids come out for swim, they are people I have never met. I am always curious why they choose to swim. I know that long before they show up, there is a thought process that has led them to this decision. Maybe they have a friend who swam, maybe they wanted to try something new and different, maybe they just heard about the trips swim take each spring, or maybe they just like to take showers. Lots of showers.

I have always wondered why Isai Valdez decided to try swimming. On numerous occasions, I would stop, ponder the question, then have to move on because I'd get a headache or become dizzy.

Throughout your four years, I have seen you ride the rollercoaster of motivation. There have been times when you have been the champion of achievement and there have been times when you have been the champion of couch potatoes worldwide. Each time I would again try to understand, the throbbing in my head would return.

One thing that was always clear in my head was your ability to lighten the moment. People like you are invaluable to the chemistry and success of a team. You provide more entertainment before breakfast than most people will experience all day. I could put a highlight reel together that would rival anything on "America's Funniest Home Videos."

I wish I could borrow you for one week in April every year. I could not anticipate, nor could you prepare, for some of the things that you have done in those weeks. You have been at your finest on our spring break trips.

In many ways, you are the classic Cathedral City Swimmer. You have worked hard for good grades and you have committed yourself to the program. You have listened and learned and you have grown into a leader. Most importantly you have been yourself.

I may not ever fully understand your motivation, but I do know that for the last four years I have appreciated it tremendously.

fleen

❖ **The View** ❖
Katie P

One of the many things I enjoy so much about my travels in the summers are the views I see. Mountains, cities, oceans, people, they all provide me with some incredible pictures. As a high school teacher and coach, I am also privileged to see kids from a variety of perspectives. From my teacher ledge; I see promise, intellect, and achievement. Ironically enough, I see some of those same qualities as a coach, but from a much different perspective. As a coach, it is almost as if we have a magnified view of everything. We see the good, the strange, and the car wrecks.

The few years you have been in the program you have provided me with many views. Some have been jaw-dropping amazing, and yes, some have been car wrecks. We all have car wrecks, it is one of the reasons we have insurance. We don't plan them, they just sort of happen. Oddly enough the good things happen pretty much the same way. The views from these moments are generally reflective and obvious.

As a student, you have provided me with a remarkable view. They talk about people having the "it factor." That special something we wish we all had. Well, you have it. You are so naturally intelligent, it makes everyone else envious. I am amazed by your ability to analyze and reason. Although I know it is not, it appears effortless.

As an athlete, strangely enough, my view is not much different. Smart people do well in my sports. They can understand concepts and only need to gain experience in order to be successful. I don't think you have come close to realizing your potential. In terms of high school sports, you just ran out of time.

I am excited to see you continue to show your view to the world. And even though you may crash the car every now and then, I believe you have an incredible insurance policy inside you. It is called the "it factor".

fleen

❖ The Big Picture ❖
Laura V

For as long as I can remember, I have been a fan of two things; sports and the underdog. Sports to me are life's extra teacher, extra parent, and extra friend. They are the avenue by which we create much of who we are. There are so many lessons we learn that we can only learn through sports. The underdog is the ultimate sports junky. They are the ones who probably appreciate what athletics can do for a person more than anyone else. They understand what sports are all about.

They understand the big picture. Laura V, I believe you understand the big picture.

High school sports, to me, are the purest form of athletics available. Kids are not paid, the term "student/athlete" really means something, they participate because they want to, and desire is more important than ability. You embody everything I feel is important in high school sports; commitment, passion, determination, and leadership. Throughout your four years of swimming, you have represented each of these qualities.

While coaches at other schools may cut athletes, you are one of the reasons I will never cut anyone. You have come to understand my philosophy about what a student/ athlete symbolizes. You have worked hard in the classroom. You have trusted your coaches. You have sacrificed to improve your ability and you have encouraged your teammates. I am honored as a coach by athletes who understand that sports are more than just about winning and losing. They understand the big picture.

As a coach, I can not think of a single lesson you have not learned that I feel is important. It is because of this that I think you will have tremendous success as you prepare for the next phase of your life.

To me, your biggest achievement in high school sports is not a certain win or a certain time, but the memories you have created and the lessons you have learned. That is why I believe you understand the big picture.

fleen

❖ **The Moment** ❖
Vivian Z

Life has a tendency to go by very quickly at times. One minute you're learning the next minute you're leaving. It is because of these times that fate has a way of introducing us to something called "a moment." A moment is many things. It is a place where time stands still. It is a place where your vision is never better and your hindsight never worse. It is a place where clarity of thought is not clouded or compromised. It is a place where complexity does not live. It can make your heart stop. A moment can change you in an instant. This is where I met you.

I remember your first race ever as a freshman. I'm sure you were planning to swim JV in an easy event, but I had other ideas. You swam varsity in a difficult one. I almost feel a little cheated as I was not the only one who witnessed your "moment." Everyone on deck saw you stop and hyperventilate. Maybe it was your unabashed attempts at garnering the affection of a few of the Maryland athletes. The swimmer, the basketball player, the…I should probably stop.

Fortunately, you would have many more. The smile on your face when, after encouraging a teammate, you saw them swim an incredible race. The motherly times when you helped me look after "the kids." The times I witnessed you deep in thought, knowing you were struggling inside. The joy you brought to sad tired faces after difficult practices. The laughter you created on bus rides and the weary eyes of an exhausted warrior.

These are but a few of the "moments" that I will remember because it was at these moments that I really felt like I knew you. It was these moments when I saw you most clearly. It will be these moments that I will remember about you. It will also be these moments that I will miss.

The wonderful thing about moments is that they can never be changed; you can only make new ones. I have no doubt that even though we may not see each other as often, we will continue to share moments.

fleen

Chapter Seven

2007

Dear Friend,

Many of you who know me know that I am a fan of sports and competition. I think it can teach us so much about life. If you were ever an athlete you know what I'm talking about. Think back on your athletic career and recall the numerous times you took the lessons you learned through sports and applied them to your life.

Remember the time you were injured and couldn't participate and how it made you appreciate the opportunities you were given. Remember the days when you just didn't have it, and you worked hard anyway knowing that continuing to work hard was still the only real option. Remember the feeling of accomplishment when you were part of a team that was committed to and achieved a season long goal. Remember the teammates you maybe didn't get along with, but still had to practice and sacrifice with each day to help reach a common goal. There is no better accidental teacher of life lessons than sports.

As you also may remember, I do not have an aquatics background. How a collegiate baseball player and professional triathlete ends up teaching life lessons through swimming is for another time. The bottom line is I feel so lucky to be doing what I do each day. And I have you all to thank for that. Your consistent support of the athletes in my program allows me to be that teacher of life lessons.

Take the JV girls team for instance. There is no better stage to teach about never giving up than with this team. To say they could swim would be like saying Paris Hilton can cook. They have both seen it happen, but probably couldn't do it themselves. Unlike Paris Hilton, my girls actually wanted to learn how. And learn how they did. A 10-2 season, best times almost every meet, quickly learning that being a swimmer at Cathedral City is about more than going fast. They would come to understand that if you don't like the journey, you won't appreciate the destination. I am proud to say they thoroughly enjoyed both. Swimmers like Katy K, Anne A, Monica R, and Veronica G would represent the vast array of ability levels. What they all had in common was the intense desire to get better and have fun at the same time.

The varsity girls and boys teams would bring new meaning to the word dichotomy. The girls would again redefine the meaning of "team" by winning 10 of 12 meets, many against teams with year-round club swimmers. The boys on the other hand would finish 2-9 and lose to many teams without club swimmers due to the fact that we only had seven boys on our team. The girls didn't always win each race, but their incredible depth allowed them to win many meets. The boys would often win every race they entered only to lose the meet due to lack of depth. The girls did not win any events at DVL. The boys won two events at DVL and finished in the top 3 in 5 other events. The girls qualified three relays for CIF and swam all three. The boys qualified all three, but could only swim two because they didn't have enough guys to swim the third. The girls would qualify three girls in one event each at CIF. The boys would qualify three boys in two events and a 4th in one. None of the girls would qualify to swim at CIF Finals on the 2nd day. All five boys would qualify *to swim the 2nd day to lead the team to an overall 9th place finish. It is only the 2nd time the boys have finished in the top ten at CIF. Jay F would become the first swimmer to represent Cathedral City at the Masters meet, a meet 2 days after CIF Finals that brings together the fastest swimmers from all four divisions. After barely qualifying in 24th out of a field of 25, Jay would finish 17th.*

As you can see the varsity girls and boys teams both had tremendous accomplishment filled seasons. Senior Andrianna M would finally qualify for CIF in the 100 breaststroke after narrowly missing the CIF cut a year ago. Sophomore Jenny R surprisingly qualified 31st out of 32 in the 100 fly. After a fantastic swim, she would finish 22nd. Jenny just learned how to swim last year…period. Madisyn B's goal was to just go to CIF her senior year. She was able to swim on all three CIF relays.

Kyle K, who didn't even qualify for CIF a year ago, would come back the 2nd day in both the 50 & 100 free and finish 14th and 11th respectively. Perhaps the most amazing story is the one about the first year kid who, having never swum before, qualifies for CIF. What makes the story even better is that he qualified to swim the 2nd day at Finals. I have never seen this happen before in all my years *of coaching. Junior Adam M, the water polo MVP of the DVL as a goalie, was simply amazing as he progressed throughout the season. The only way I can describe him is "freak of nature!"*

It is not hard to imagine why I enjoy not only teaching anatomy at Cathedral City, I enjoy teaching life. I just happen to do it from the deck of a pool each day and they call me coach.

Thank you again for your unwavering support of Cathedral City Swim.

Swimmingly

❖ The Mirror ❖
Amber H

When I started this letter I felt like the author with writer's block who begins the story, but is unable to find the next word. Behind him lies a pile of wadded up paper as a testament to his ineptness. I cannot tell you how many times I began this letter. What I think I can tell you is why it was so difficult. What I have told you and many others is: "that there are many people you can fool in life, but the one person you cannot fool is the person staring back at you in the mirror."

What made this so difficult for me was how much of myself I see in you. When I met you, you, were not very athletic, but you were energetic. School was not a priority, but you excelled in the subjects that interested you. Many people knew you and liked your zaniness, but few you could call true friends.

Over the course of the last few years, I hope you have grown to discover the same things in yourself, that I have come to know. First and foremost, you are athletically gifted. I am amazed at your natural ability to move so gracefully through the water. What you have achieved through water polo, and your ability to make a CIF cut in swim, is exceptional. Having amazingly huge hands and feet doesn't hurt.

I believe you also have the ability to inspire. While you may not think so, many people watch you and are drawn by your passion. Passion has a way of making its way to the head of the line without trying. People cannot hide things that are meaningful to them. You have never been able to hide the things you've cared about, which is one of the reasons you have always been honest with me.

Finally, you are sincere to a fault. What makes you unique is that you are sincere in your strengths and also in your weaknesses. You are not always sensitive to those around you, but it is not because you don't care, it's mostly because you are not aware. Yet I have seen you be the most uplifting soul, encouraging others when they felt like stopping. You have demonstrated your lack of patience in yourself many, many times. What has amazed me is, when it comes to teaching others the things that are important to you, you seem to find and reveal this unlimited source of patience.

When you leave this room tonight, you will be faced with many choices that will shape your future. It is my hope that as you learn more about yourself, you realize the incredible potential for good that exists in you, that you never forgot to surround yourself with visionary people, and that you are not afraid to put yourself out there to be exposed for others to see who you really are. It is then, and only then, that you will become the person you were created to be. Then when you look in the mirror, someone will be smiling back at you.

fleen

❖ **The X-File** ❖
Andrianna M

I love the X-Files. The unexplained phenomenon. The inexplicable talent. For these are all you. I have seen many kids over the years: some with amazing talent, some with a little talent, and some who couldn't spell talent. You are an X-File in many ways. I should have known after your brother did so well in just one season that you would follow suit. I should have known that you would be so committed to school. I should have known that you would be so dedicated to swim. You have gifts that many wish they had.

I would have to jog my memory to remember an athlete, with your talent, who would look so bad at the beginning of the season and so good at the end. Year after year, I was so pleased with your progress at the end of the season, and then the next season would begin, and I felt I was looking at a different person. I would cringe as I watched you swim in February. It was like watching Bambi learning to walk. I found myself asking "how did she ever go that fast last year?' As usual, you would transform yourself into that amazing talent again by the end of the year.

The last few years I would just laugh at your early season workouts. Others would ask, "is this her first year?" Oddly enough, I could not pinpoint the moment of your transformation. I would look for it, but would always miss it. Just the X-File in you I guess.

I have always been proud of your commitment to school. To hear you talk about classes, projects, and even teachers who frustrated you was fun for me. For I knew that you were more than just an athlete, you cared about learning.

I also appreciated your willingness to have fun and involve others. I never saw you as a person who only hung out with certain people. I saw you as a teammate in the truest sense of the word. It was a joy to see you encouraging, laughing, working, and always with a smile. The fact that the team viewed you as one of the hardest workers on the team was not a surprise to me.

I am grateful to you for giving so much of yourself to swim over the past four years. I can not thank you enough. I look forward to hearing about how much fun you are having in college, how much you are learning, and how much the X-File in you is being exhibited.

fleen

❧ **The Question** ❧
Danielle G

Athletes fear me. I'd like to think it is a healthy fear. I don't fear many athletes, but I must admit that I fear you. I fear you for the same reason other athletes fear me. Because neither of us wants to hear those simple three words. "Can we talk?"

When I ask the question, it could be good or bad. When you ask the question, I wait for the other shoe to drop, because it is generally not good news. Not many people know the trials you have gone through in your four years of high school. I won't list them now, but I think it is safe to say that they are not part of a normal high school experience.

Early on I saw you as a committed, hard-working, fun-loving, and caring person. You are exactly what swim is about. I could see you improving and more importantly, enjoying your experience. Then the question came, followed by "I am moving to another city". My heart sank. Then you said it was local and you could still attend Cathedral City. I was overjoyed. Then you said "if..." Any statement followed by "if", usually doesn't have a good finish. Yet somehow you made it work.

Then the question came again followed by "I am moving to another city, (pause for effect) in northern California". Saying goodbye to you was not easy. I could sense you didn't want to go. I didn't want you to go. I was sad that circumstances beyond your control made your decision for you.

Then one day your mom showed up in my classroom after school, followed shortly thereafter by you. I'm sure you remember how surprised I was to see you again. I didn't know how to react. I was just thrilled the simple three words you uttered were, "I'm moving back".

Danielle, you are a woman of resilience. You know it and I know it. I can't remember ever using that word to describe an athlete before. Look up resilience in the dictionary and you will find a quality that almost everyone wishes they had. For it is this quality that fuels goals, knowledge, and emotions.

Thank you for being such a quality person, an encouragement to others, and a member of my swim family.

fleen

❖ **Just Because** ❖
Delanie B

To paraphrase Shakespeare, "'Tis not me to understand why people swim. For the mind of a high school student is like the depths of the sea." I think I know what he meant, no one has the equipment to go that deep, and even if they did, they would probably be afraid of what they might find. I remember you telling me that the reason you joined water polo was because as you were having lunch in my room, we were about to start our polo meeting, and you didn't want to go outside because it was hot. After that, it didn't matter to me why you decided to swim.

Everyone possesses gifts and talents. I have seen many over the course of my coaching career. I place you in a select group of people who have the gift of levity. You have the ability to turn any situation into a question mark. You are one of the only people I know that I can have a conversation with and have more questions at the end than I did at the beginning. You spent one whole road trip trying to come up with your own "oxymoron." (big/little fish is not an oxymoron by the way)

And you have some of the most unique dance moves I have ever seen.

You are the type of athlete who makes swim fun for me. You are the reason I will never cut anyone from the team. I loved watching you race, and enjoyed it even more when you learned how to compete. It was an adventure to watch you learn the cheers and even more enjoyable to see you mess them up. It was fun to see you practice something and then finally see yourself doing it the right way. It made me proud to see you stay in the water and shake someone's hand at the end of your races.

The fact that you are not afraid to be you is probably your greatest strength. You would think more people would understand this. While many people are altering themselves as a result of their surroundings, you have always remained true.

Remember, it does not matter that you are the last in a group to understand the situation, it is irrelevant that you don't know what an oxymoron is, and more people should learn to sing and dance like you. What you already know is that it is important to be yourself and "just because" is reason enough sometimes.

Thank you for investing in swim and making me smile so much this season.

fleen

❖ I knew ❖
Federica C

I love exchange students. I love the fact that they think they know what it will be like to live and learn in America. They have TV and the internet. They have seen "The O.C." and MTV's "The Real World." As an American, I hate to admit that some of those stereotypes exist in various forms, especially in California. Having spent many years in Europe, I also had an idea of what life in America would be like for Federica C.

Even before I met you I knew you. When you arrived in the home of a swimmer/water polo player, I can imagine the first few thoughts in your head; why does your room smell so funny? Why do you wear a swimsuit in all your pictures? You get up at <u>what time</u> to practice? And you do it again after school? You don't know what Nutella is? As you pondered these questions, I knew your life would never be the same.

Even before I met you, I knew you. I knew your accent would immediately endear you to people, I knew your expressive open personality would make you many friends, and I knew you would wonder "why?"…a lot. And I knew you knew this. I also knew your life would never be the same.

Even before the team met you I knew they would love you. We loved you at your best and worst moments. We loved you when you missed your race, we loved you when you became a walking zombie at school after morning practice, we loved you when you got that crazy "pain in your chest and couldn't "brieve", we loved you when you tried to cheer on the bus and messed up the words, we loved you when you set a time goal and then worked hard to achieve it, and we loved you because we knew your life would never be the same.

Even before I met you I knew you. I knew you would quickly learn that swimming is not a team sport at Cathedral City, it's a family sport. You became a part of all of us. Even though many of us may never see you again, I want to assure you that because you are now family, I will see you again. And when I see you we will sip espresso, look at pictures, share stories and laugh. Finally, I will smile knowing that both of our lives will never be the same.

fleen

❖ **The Name** ❖
Livier V

Can you imagine life without a name? When you stop to think about it, everything has a name. We name our kids, our pets, our cars, our toys, I even know people who name their BBQ. For some, the name is almost paramount to their existence. Someone once told me I didn't look like a Brad, she wanted to name me Boo. To this day she still calls me Boo. I don't even know what a Boo is, but I do know who I am.

Livier is a beautiful name. You are, and probably will be, the only Livier I will ever know. How unique a name, how individual an identity, how unforgettable a title. If I had a daughter I would consider naming her Livier, but I'm afraid it just wouldn't work with Fleener.

Velazquez. Again a beautiful name...anyway you spell it. Herein lies the irony. I have known you for 4 years and have spelled your last name probably 10 different ways. I have spelled it wrong on team rosters, team trips, and even team equipment. I even spelled it wrong this year, your SENIOR year. I'll even admit I spelled it wrong in this letter the first time.

I hope that you (and your mother) realize that however I spell your name; it is not what you are. The name, although important, does not reflect your kindness, it does not reveal your serenity, and it does not epitomize your determination. It also does not disclose your dancing, party girl, wild side, divulge your talent for misplacing everything or disclose the fact that you are blind as a bat.

There are many things I admire about you that are not revealed in your name. You know who you are. You are sincere. You are honest. You are a woman with a genuine spirit. You have a heartfelt disposition.

I may spell your name wrong again in the future, but I promise you I will not forget what it represents.

fleen

❖ **The Impression** ❖
Madisyn B

Some of the most difficult and joyous times come when we transition from one phase of our lives to another. A 16th birthday, a graduation, a marriage, or having to say goodbye to someone you care about, we struggle to put the moment into perspective. It doesn't even matter if we know when the time will come; it is still hard to prepare for. In times like these, we're often left thinking about the legacy we will leave, the bonds we've formed, and the impressions we have made.

Four years ago you joined swim mainly because a friend encouraged you to join with her. Throughout that year you unknowingly began leaving your impression on me. I noticed many things about you that year. First, you had an uncanny ability to fall asleep anywhere, anytime, on anyone or anything. Friend, stranger, pole, it didn't matter. The sporadic drooling just made the instant more memorable. Secondly, you learned quickly. It was because you wanted to learn, not because you were especially gifted. Whether it was school, swim, or friends, you became skilled at achieving a goal because it was important to you. Thirdly, you have one of the most uninspiring appetites I have ever seen. I mean seriously, can one truly survive on chicken fingers alone? Finally, you established yourself as a woman of character by the way you treated other people. You were considerate, kind, and encouraging and it didn't hurt that you were just plain goofy.

What makes this moment especially difficult for me is that over the course of the last three years, all you have done is left a deeper impression. You have done nothing except be yourself and that is why I can't believe I am writing this letter to you tonight. You have not wavered, you have not faltered, you have not compromised, and you have not cheated yourself.

While many are constantly trying to be the flavor of the week, you are like spumoni ice cream; no one really knows what flavor it is, but people like it because it sounds intriguing, it looks different, and people are left trying to figure out what it was long after it has been digested. It has left an impression.

Madisyn B, you have left your impression on Cathedral City swim and on me. Both are better because of you and both will always remember you.

fleen

❖ **One More Time** ❖
Triny R

I will be the first to admit that swimming is typically not near the top of the list of sports to try in high school. Students aren't often introduced to competitive swimming at a young age. Many grow up playing softball, basketball, volleyball, or in your case soccer. This is naturally what they gravitate to in high school. Yet there you were your freshman year giving water polo a go. And there you were a few days later deciding that yes, soccer was the sport for you.

I did not know you well then. It is difficult to form that life bond in a few short days. Many things happen over the course of a high school experience. Friends change, attitudes change, and interests change. Fast forward to your senior year and Triny R decides to give water polo another try, and ultimately swim as well.

I must admit I was a little surprised you wanted to try it again. I knew you found the sport difficult three years earlier and I knew that it would still be difficult three years later. What I did not know was how determined and confident you were in your demeanor. Over the years I have found that desire, work ethic, and a positive attitude can take you a long way, not just in sports, but in life as well. You most certainly exhibit all three qualities.

You seemed to know it would be difficult but had decided long before it began that you would not quit again. When you finished polo and wanted to swim, I was thrilled. Your personality is a lot like mine. Serious in what you do, not so serious in who you are. This is what makes you a good friend and an enjoyable person to be around.

You appear to know your strengths as well as your limitations. It was a pleasure for me to see you putting your best effort into these two characteristics. This is why I believe you were so successful this year. It is also why you will be successful in college and beyond. I am glad you decided to swim. I am even happier to say that you will always be a part of the swim family at Cathedral City.

fleen

Chapter Eight

2008

Dear Friend,

They work so hard it hurts. They sacrifice time with friends to pursue a goal that many would consider meaningless. They wake up at a time when most people are still dreaming. They swim before and after school, 3 1/2 hours a day. After school when most students go home, they go to another classroom to study more. They arrive home tired and hungry, yet know they still have more to do before it all begins again…tomorrow.

<u>What have you done today?</u>

They arrive as clay and are molded into people of true character, accomplished athletes, and humble men and women. They learn more because they care to learn more. Most will never swim past high school, yet all would never trade the experience for anything.

What have you become?

They help their teammates with homework, motivation, and courage. They discover a world beyond Cathedral City, beyond California. They make history and learn about history, not just in a classroom, but in the pool and across the country. They have created lifetime friendships and memories.

What have you learned?

In the span of three short months, a team of beginners and experienced student/athletes; once again transformed themselves into something even they had a difficult time recognizing. As a coach, I am able to watch this transformation from average student to above average and from novice to accomplished swimmer. I am constantly amazed at the change my team goes through each season. Some might think it is unusual, but it is not. It happens every year. Even though the faces are new, the end result is the same.

The girls' team was once again filled with many kids who began high school with no swimming background. Once again they managed to win meet after meet with their depth. With no club simmers, they worked hard to improve each hour, each day, each week. At the end of the season, their efforts were rewarded. Junior Rachel F would battle through injury all season to win the 100 Fly & 200 IM at the Desert Valley League Championships. She would also swim the 200 IM & 500 Free at CIF as well as swim on the 400 Free Relay team. Sophomore Melanie H would experience an up and down season that ended with a CIF qualifying time in the 500 Free. Both Melanie H and Rachel F would also swim their best splits on the 400 Free Relay. Rachel, Melanie, and junior Jenny R would go 1, 2, 3 in the 100 Fly at DVL. The CIF qualifying relay would need to add a last minute replacement, yet still dropped four seconds at CIF. These things don't happen by accident. They happen because these girls worked hard to earn their success. What makes this group of girls unique is that there are no seniors.

The boys' team would, for the first time in almost ten years, field a full team of thirteen boys. As a result, they would win more meets (8) than any team before them. They would also see an incredible culmination to the careers of four seniors, Jay F, Kyle K, Michael P, and Adam M. Gone were the memories of winning every race in a dual meet only to lose the meet because of depth issues. Kyle K would never lose a race all season. Jay F would only lose once, and that was to a teammate. Kyle K would finally break the School Record in the 50 Free with a time of 22.10. Jay F would break his own School Record in the 200 IM by swimming the 5th fastest time at CIF, 1:59.85. At CIF Jay F, Kyle K, Adam M, and junior Brandon F would place 3rd in the 200 Medley Relay after being seeded 12th with a time of 1:41.88, just missing the School Record. In the 200 Free Relay they were seeded 14th yet Jay F, Kyle K, Adam M, and Michael P would break their own School Record by over two seconds to finish 5th with a time of 1:30.81. Kyle K would finish 7th and 9th in the 100 Free and 50 Free respectively. Jay F would also finish 7th in the 100 Breast. Adam M would finish 13th in the same event. As a team, the boys placed 7th, the highest finish in school history. The boys knew they needed to be at their best at CIF and they never wavered in their pursuit. While other DVL schools were struggling to swim their best times, every boys swim was a season best. As a coach, I couldn't have been more proud of the boys and girls teams.

Spring Break was quite a week. Swimming indoors was a new experience for all. They quickly learned that the chlorine stench stays with you a little longer when you swim indoors. Subways were another adventure. Discovering Boston has the oldest subway system in the U.S. came as no shock to anyone. While most passengers read or listened to music, our kids were going back and forth between subway surfing and sleeping. Seeing firsthand the sites associated with our founding fathers was also a treat for everyone. They learned that seeing history in person is much more interesting than reading about it in books. Visiting Simmons College, where the team trained, gave them a different perspective to the small college experience. They also saw the other side with visits to Harvard and M.I.T. What an opportunity for the team to visit these historic universities.

As another season and school year comes to an end, I want to thank you again for providing me the chance to impact the lives of this special group. Your generous contributions have made it possible for these student-athletes to grow and learn so much about themselves in three short months.

Swimmingly

❖ **The Freak** ❖
Adam M

We should all be so lucky. We should all be so blessed. To be given the tools necessary to do those things we choose. For many it is a labor of love, it does not come naturally. Some must work twice as hard to achieve what comes easily to others. This is not you. For some reason, you have been anointed, dusted with promise, blessed with potential. Simply put, you are a freak of nature. We should all be so lucky.

A freak. An anomaly. An irregularity. That is what you are. I have called you these names many times. It's the coaching term I use when I can't take credit for my coaching. When other coaches would inquire about the new breaststroker I would just say, "He is a Freak of Nature". Not knowing how to respond, they would just smile, nod, and then walk away. I know why they did this; it was because they wish they had a Freak of Nature on their team as well.

In all my years of coaching, I have only run across a few like you. You're like an endangered species that is seldom seen, that rare breed of animal that some search for their entire life. Once discovered, you're like the prize catch to be put on display for others to view. I should have charged admission for others to come watch you in your natural habitat, the pool.

I quickly learned that with the label of "Freak" comes the realization that there are some other abnormal behaviors, AKA quirks if you will. First is the ability to be relatively one dimensional. It was pretty much breaststroke or no stroke. Although your freestyle did improve, I can't take credit for it (nor would I want to) because it was more or less, self-taught. Watching you swim freestyle I often wondered if your arms knew each other because they rarely did the same thing. I also wondered if your legs were detachable. Some days I saw them and other days I didn't. Some days I only saw one, which I just brushed off as the whole "Freak of Nature" thing. As a coach, it was a great way of explaining to others what I couldn't understand myself. The second quirk took me a while to realize. At various times in practice, most people would rest on the wall. For some reason you rested on the lane line some five feet from the wall. I soon learned that you were sort of resting, mostly relieving. Freaks of Nature must have small bladders.

It has been a pleasure watching you in your natural habitat these last two years. I hope you realize your "Freak" status is not limited to the pool. You are funny, good-natured, smart, and gifted in many ways other than athletics. I can't wait to find out, many years from now, what you have done with your gifts.

fleen

❖ **The Battery** ❖
Jay F

There is a famous commercial about a bunny rabbit and a battery. The punchline is that it keeps going and going and going. You are much like this battery. There have been many things and people that have come and gone, but you have been one of the cornerstones of the last four years. You have been a pleasure to most of your teachers, you have been an example of hard work to your teammates, and you have been a joy to coach. When you arrived I had an idea of what I was going to get, and yet I knew that I would be surprised.

I knew your sisters were committed, hard-working, intelligent, with a sense of humor that was just off the edge. You have not disappointed. Dependability is an outstanding quality to have and you are the poster child. What an amazing feeling as a coach to never question an athlete's commitment.

You worked unquestionably hard every day. I felt at times that I didn't work you hard enough. That became apparent the more we used heart rate as an indicator of effort. I could rarely get your heart to the anaerobic threshold. It became a bit of a challenge for me sometimes to see how much I could push you. It is fun to coach someone who enjoys training. I'm so excited for you because I know you will excel in college.

I have had many student-athletes over the years who have felt they knew more than their teachers. It was usually just an excuse for a poor performance in class. You on the other hand I believe at times do know more than some of your teachers. I hate to admit that, but it's comically true. I also enjoyed having conversations with you because when we had a difference of opinion you never backed down. I only knew that I won when you threw knowledge into a completely different topic.

One thing I learned very early in your career is that you never miss anything. You know exactly what is going on and just wait for the right moment to pounce, which is why you are the best Fleen impersonator on the planet. You pull out comments even I had forgotten. I also learned early on that, like your sisters, you are a physical anomaly on land. It's a nice way of saying you work well in water. Whether it was an ankle, elbow, wrist, or kidney, you always managed to come up with a new way to injure yourself.

I will miss watching you interact with freshman girls; I will miss watching you dominate arguments with knowledge the opposition knew nothing of; I will miss watching you step up to the challenge in every race that meant something; most of all I will miss watching you on a daily basis demonstrate your commitment to the things you truly enjoy.

fleen

❖ **The Missing Link** ❖
Kyle K

For some it is a mystery what their letter will be titled. I'm sure that for you it was no doubt. You cemented that legacy in Santa Barbara your freshman year. How someone can sprint through the sand on their hands and feet as fast as they can run on two legs is not natural. Over the last four years, you have done more than a few things that have left me shaking my head in disbelief. Some good, some bad, but always vintage Kyle. These letters are always part remembering, part thank you, and part lesson.

I remember your freshman year. I heard you had played polo...kind of. I was told you only played on the defensive side because you couldn't swim back and forth with the game. How excited was I to have that kind of talent come out for swim? I was told you were not massive. Just what I was looking for in a new swimmer! I found out you were not friends with the books. Just what I needed, another project! You really should thank the girl with the family issues I allowed to swim that year. Having done so, I felt I had to offer you the same 2nd chance. Who would have thought four years later you would leave the fastest sprinter in school history, be part of the most wins and highest CIF placing for a boy's team, and grow into a good practice swimmer? To call you a good practice swimmer your first three years would be like calling Paris Hilton a good actress. She might believe it, but everyone else knows better.

I want to thank you for growing into a tremendous teammate. You have always been a person who gets along and includes everyone. That quality is at the core of this program. Those that understand this let nothing get in their way and consistently achieve more. You have done this. Those that don't will always live with the excuses they invent. You have come to learn and represent many of the important principles of Cathedral City Swim; selflessness, sportsmanship, not taking yourself too seriously, and above all having fun. When the team needed a moment of levity you were more than willing to answer the call. You have held close and fostered the traditions of this program when others were waiting for someone to step up. For this, I can't thank you enough.

You have learned many lessons in your four years. One, you can't always do things on your own. At times you must trust and believe in the wisdom of others. Two, talent and potential should never be taken for granted. I cannot put into words the joy you will experience in life when you maximize both. Finally, never forget the conversation we had before CIF. I shared with you two versions for the future of Kyle K. Both were realistic, one had a much better ending. Please allow me to tell that story.

fleen

❖ The Vision ❖
Malita P

When most students enter high school they have many things on their mind; you had one. When some were thinking about which classes to take, you already knew. When others didn't have a vision of the future, yours was like a picture, painted and sold. When your friends were talking about what could be; you were talking about what would be. When I speak of senior athletes I am proud of the influence that swim has had on their lives. When I speak of you it is because of the influence you have had on swim.

Not many freshmen come to high school with visions of college, let alone Harvard. You were clearly different. To hear you talk about your goals that year was both eyebrow raising and inspiring. As time went by your vision never wavered. You impressed me with your knowledge of what was necessary to achieve your goal at every turn. Whether it was academically, athletically, community service, or leadership related, you knew what was required and took the necessary steps. At times it was humorous to watch others react to your plans for high school and beyond. On the outside they probably said "yeah that sounds cool", but on the inside were thinking "yeah right, let's just go to the mall." The funny thing is you probably still went to the mall and just stayed up later doing your homework.

I can honestly say I don't think I've met anyone like you before. I wouldn't say you and I are particularly close, but I have always been impressed by your focus. You have a nature that exudes whim and zaniness, which is perfect for our team, but you never compromised your goal-driven aspirations.

You have some unique attributes. You have a deep relationship with style and fashion, but please don't ever straighten your hair again. You have an uncanny ability to "grind" at the thought of your favorite song. You both crave and shun the spotlight. You have this grave face whenever you're about to ask (tell) me something you think I don't want to hear. You understand that knowledge is empowering. I enjoyed the times we discussed important ideas even though we may have had a difference of opinion.

As you know, Roz and I had a bet about the talent potential of you and Kyle your freshman year. Based on what we saw that first day, Roz chose Kyle, I chose you. Little did we know that four years later we would both be right. Kyle's school record is evidence of her choice. I chose you because I saw something more than just your swimming potential, I saw your drive, I saw your heart, I saw your vision. The good news is you are just beginning to realize your potential and I will always be watching to see how.

Thank you for being such a shining example to younger swimmers. Know that many stories will be told of Michael P to future swimmers. Some will be funny, others will be serious, all will be inspiring.

fleen

Chapter Nine

2009

Dear Friend,

Swimming is one of those sports that many don't recognize until the Olympics come along once every four years. Then someone, if you're lucky, becomes a rock star overnight (See Michael Phelps) Kobe Bryant is now a fan of swimming (he was probably in the stands wondering "the sidestroke must be next?"), some undersized gymnast thinks you're hot (must be the ears), and a middle-aged man in Kentucky just jumped in his backyard pool for the first time in years (he quickly got out because the water color in his pool looked nothing like the water color of the pool in Beijing). Swimming is notorious for its, well, um, un...notoriety. The idea of staring at a black line and two black T's doesn't exactly spell money. For heaven's sake, you're so wet you don't even know if you're sweating.

Swimming is not a glamorous sport. High school swimming is about as unglamorous as you can get. So why, at a school where nearly 80% of the population is on free or reduced lunches, where there is no pool, where a mother has to tell her 8 year old who now wants to learn how to swim because he just saw Michael Phelps win another Gold medal that there is no place to go to learn how to swim, are there kids who transform themselves into graceful swimmers, CIF qualifiers, collegiate athletes, and valedictorians? I'd probably have a different job if I knew the answer.

What I do know is 46 kids began a journey down a road and saw:

- *6 swimmers and 2 Relays qualify for CIF.*
- *An amazingly fun spring break trip to Santa Barbara.*
- *The Varsity girls lose only to a team with 5 club swimmers & an Olympian from Beijing and to the team that won CIF.*
- *A JV Boys team for the 1st time in school history.*

- *Some of the most entertaining kids on campus.*
- *A few athletes improve more in one season than I have ever seen before. Leading the way was sophomore Max Becerra who placed 16th at CIF in the 100 breast.*
- *The top two scholastic sports teams being Boys & Girls swim.*

At the end of that road is sophomore Arquin A. Arquin never swam before and was, literally, a fish out of water when he began. He was in danger of being dismissed from the team because he kept stopping to stand in the middle of the pool. To see him now you'd think he'd been swimming for years. There is freshman Johnny C. Johnny was one of those kids I thought might have only one stroke, freestyle. He would go on to be the 14th best backstroker in the DVL. There is freshman Lorrie T. We discovered she couldn't really do breaststroke or backstroke. She was taught fly and ended up swimming Varsity a few times by the end of the year, crying tears of joy (or relief) after the first time. Finally, there is senior Bree G. Bree swam for us as a freshman, did very well, and then transferred to another school in the valley. It was at this school that Bree's troubles began. After two difficult years, she transferred back and wanted *to swim again. Bree was one of the most energetic, hard-working and positive kids on the team. She would make an individual CIF qualifying time and be an important part of both qualifying relays. There are 42 other inspiring stories just like this at the end of this road.*

It is stories like these that I wish you could witness and experience for yourself. To see the struggle pay off, to see the confidence grow right before your eyes, to see lasting friendships form, this is what you help develop. Thank you again for your faithful support of Cathedral City Swimming.

Swimmingly

❖ **The Growth** ❖
Alex S

One of the joys I receive from coaching is seeing the progress athletes make as they go through the program. Winning has always meant little to me and it is one thing I try to express to my athletes. If a person does not enjoy the journey, the destination becomes hollow and meaningless. I believe you understand this.

Observing athletes as they learn about themselves develop is another aspect of my job I thoroughly enjoy. Seeing the growth in you over the last three years has constantly made me smile.

For many athletes, there is little I know about what goes on in their lives beyond what I see at school and the pool. You fit this I category perfectly. You also have the unique distinction of having started your swimming career at another high school in the valley. Being very genuine and often quiet has been your trademark. What has impressed me about you is how you have positively meshed all of these unique aspects of your life into the person you have become.

I have no doubt your parents have taught you well and are very proud of your accomplishments in school and your commitment to swim and water polo. As your coach, I know you are dependable, determined, and care deeply about those around you. While others may not realize this, I have seen these qualities become more and more a part of your character over the years. These are also the qualities, not your swimming ability, which will lead you to a bright future.

I have witnessed your confidence grow in your athletic ability, your academic ability, your laughing ability, and most importantly yourself. You are becoming exactly the person that makes me proud to coach. I am excited for you as you continue down the road to your next journey. I am confident you will gain strength with each step.

fleen

❖ **The Highs and Lows** ❖
Brandon F

In my life I have been fortunate enough to have had the chance to travel much more than I ever expected. At the end of the day, I have slept just about everywhere. I've stayed in 5 Star hotels and I've slept on the ground (both unplanned). I've slept in planes, trains, and automobiles. I was kicked awake by an angry Spanish man demanding my passport and bitten awake by an angry spider. I feel like I've witnessed the unpleasantness of the basement as well as the spoils of the penthouse suite. This is what I think we have in common. In your four years, I think you have also experienced it all.

Your freshman year everything was new and exciting. Being the new kid on the block, you just took it all in with a smile. The team split 12 meets, but would also be the first team to lose to Coachella Valley. Not having swum before, I was very pleased with your success. You worked hard and went fast when you were supposed to. You played hard and laughed even more. You survived San Diego and going to CIF had to be memorable. All the girls loved Brandon.

Your sophomore year the team would win only twice. Once again the boys would live in the shadows of the girls' success. But also once again the boys would shine at CIF. You would qualify by yourself and be an important part of two fast relays. All the girls loved Brandon.

In your junior year you would be a part of the most successful boys' team in school history. You would also realize that nothing is guaranteed. While you swam fast, a freak injury prevented you from being as fast as we both thought you would be at CIF. Still, you persevered and the girls still loved you.

This year had to be a challenge. The team was full of young promising swimmers and wins were hard to come by. You were once again derailed by a freak injury, but would still qualify for CIF and set that long-awaited school record, and the girls would still love you.

My friend, you have seen it all. Our highs do not define us and our lows do not consume us. The true test of our character is how we handle both. Your character, like everyone's before you, will be determined by what you have learned these last four years and how you apply it in the future. As you leave tonight I am confident of three things; first, that as you mature you will still be full of energy, the life of the party, and make us all proud; second, that you will grow to appreciate every moment of every day; and finally, that the girls will still love you.

fleen

❖ **The Return** ❖
Bree G

I'm not sure anyone or anything can really prepare us for our future. Maybe no one that is, except for ourselves. I will be the first to admit that the life I lead is not by my design. My plan had me pitching in the big leagues, eventually coaching baseball, living in a place where rain was not by accident, somebody would call me dad and teaching was an honorable profession… for someone else. I was clearly not good at life planning. Fortunately, my faith kept me grounded in reality and open to other ideas.

I was more devastated than you will ever know when you left after your freshman year. Here you were this eager, energetic and talented freshman. Soaking up life and giving your best, you gave your all to me and the other kids in the program. And then you left. I didn't see it coming and I fought hard to stop it. It took me a long time to accept the fact that it was not my future for you; it was your future for yourself.

I knew exactly what was happening to you at each turn you would take. I never sought information about you, but it would always arrive. It was at these times that I had to remind myself that the future was yours, not mine.

Then one day someone came to my room and asked if I saw her. Who? I said. "Bree," they replied, "She's back. She wants to swim." I think I know why we still never saw each other for months. I'm not sure either of us would know what to say.

I know what to say now. I'm proud of your commitment to me and my program, but not so much about your piercings. I'm proud that if you were apprehensive about joining swim again, you didn't show it. You worked hard, never questioned, and others noticed. I am not proud of your eating habits. I am so proud that you saw improvements in yourself. You recognized that small changes each day add up to a wonderful result. That result for you was CIF. While I am not proud of your Dr Pepper habit, I'm not sure I've ever been happier for someone making it to CIF than I was for you.

I hope as you leave here today you will continue to seek a positive future. Understand that the small choices you make every day will ultimately shape the bright future others see for you. More importantly, I hope you recognize the bright future that is already inside you.

fleen

❖ **Not Starbucks** ❖
Jackie W

As you know I like Starbucks coffee. I can rely on the fact that wherever I go I will find a Starbucks, yes even in Switzerland. I can also rest easy knowing that wherever I go the taste will never surprise me. Jackie W (and I always call you by your first and last name because I can't seem to separate the two. Like when you've done something wrong and your parents use both names together, and sometimes the middle name as well. Then you really know you're in trouble. Even your teammates call you Jackie W). You are the polar opposite of Starbucks. (Now I understand you may not know what that means right now, but I'm sure someone will explain it to you later).

There aren't many people around like Jackie W, and also unlike Starbucks, you continue to amaze me with the things that come out of your mouth. I will explain something short and easy to comprehend, then when I'm finished, you will ask me a question about the very thing I just said. It's almost like I never said it before. One day after I said something, you paused, looked at me and said, in your classic Jackie W style, "Mista Fleena, you'z a ho." Everyone around didn't know how to react, then realizing *you* had said it, just began laughing.

I was disappointed when you didn't swim your junior year. Partly because you had done fairly well the previous year, but mostly because you are a living, breathing, Whoopie cushion and I missed that. Who doesn't laugh when they sit on one? I don't know who was more excited that you chose to swim again, me, or everyone else who remembered Jackie W from the year before. You are a little bit like a car crash, you don't want to look at it, but you can't help yourself. Unlike a car crash, you make people laugh after they see you.

Everyone knows that once you're in the swim family that is Cathedral City, you are in it for life. I can't wait to get together with you in the future and catch up, talk about what you're doing now, and meet your family. Because even though you may be married with kids, as we say our goodbyes, your family will be shouting from the car, "Hurry up, let's go Jackie W!"

fleen

❖ Call 911
Jenny R

You are truly one of a kind in every sense of the word. There are so many words that describe you, that if I told them to people, they'd think I was talking about 10 completely different people. Dichotomy does not begin to describe you. Stubborn, yet level headed. Lazy, yet determined. Clueless, yet thoughtful. Athletically gifted, yet eternally clumsy.

These are but a few of the many adjectives that translate into Jenny R. I'm not sure I've ever met someone like you before. I had to call in my alumni o talk to you when you didn't want to hear the important truth come from me. Personally, I think you knew what you were going to do all along but just liked to watch me sweat it out.

I really believe you to be one of the athletes that have made me the most proud and the most frustrated in a four-year period. I can't remember anyone making such an enormous transformation between their freshman and sophomore year as you. You will forever be the poster child for someone who wants to improve so much that they just will themselves to be better. No one has ever improved as much in polo or swim as you did that year. Your desire, drive, and determination were off the charts. As a result, you became a force, an example, and a leader for all to see.

You dealt with many issues outside of sports that might have derailed others, but you didn't let it derail you. You could have let silly high school issues change your focus, but you didn't. You could have decided that I knew nothing and you knew everything, but you kept an open mind. You have a propensity for the freak injury and could have chosen to live in a bubble, but you decided to play tennis your senior year and were MVP.

I will remember so much about you, some of it strange, but most of it inspirational. I honestly think I will tell more stories about Jenny R. than I will about any former athlete, both good and bad, but mostly good. Except for the time when you….I'll save that story for another time.

I know at times you didn't like to hear the words I said, but thank you for listening. Thank you for remembering what was ultimately most important and keeping the right perspective during those tough times outside the pool. Thank you for laying your heart and soul on the line for me and your teammates when you were injured. Thank you for remaining true to yourself.

Remember that I will always be here for you, but somehow I know that at those times you will see my face, hear my voice, and already know what I will tell you.

fleen

❖ **The Choice** ❖
Jessica R

As a teacher and coach I have learned there are important traits to possess; confidence, a thick skin, perspective, and the ability to laugh. I am always and never amazed. I expect the impossible, but am never surprised when I see it. I am consistently yet rarely rewarded. When you chose water polo and swim, you didn't have a choice of coaches, I was it. When you chose to take anatomy, you didn't have a choice of teachers, I was it. When you chose to put your complete faith and trust in me as a person, you had a choice, but it was me who was amazed, surprised, and rewarded. Many kids have had an impact on me, but none like you. I think I have learned more from you than you will ever realize.

There was nothing in your background that said you would end up being an amazing water polo player, an incredible swimmer, and an accomplished student. Even I had reservations about your ability after your freshman year, but like you did when you entered high school, you chose to put yourself in situations that you knew would make you better and stronger as a student, an athlete, and person. In fact, the more I learned about you, the more impressed I became with your achievements.

I have seen so many kids, with so much more opportunity given to them, accomplish little. You on the other hand are like MacGyver, you can do anything with a pen, a polo ball, a kickboard, and some chewing gum. You have never let setbacks or heartache deter you. You have learned the right perspective that sports can teach, that nothing worth having comes easily, and you learned all this while never compromising your integrity.

You have given me so much to be proud of, so much to laugh about, and you have taught me so much over the last four years. Thank you for your <u>many</u> words and notes of thanks. They have meant a lot to me and have always seemed to arrive at the right time. Thank you for your effort in school and practice, you have been more of an example to others than you will ever know. Thank you for your cheers, your encouraging words to teammates, and your screams. No one can scream like you! Finally, thank you for teaching me so much about you and about myself. Part of me will miss you very much next year, another part will be so anxious to see you continue to blossom. Please remember that in me you will always find a coach and teacher, but more importantly, you will always find someone who cares about you very much.

fleen

❖ **The Name** ❖
Gardenia (Smalls) R

They say you can tell a lot about someone from their name. When people meet you, then learn your nickname, I think most people get it. The swim program has a history of creating names for people. This year alone we have an Egg Roll, a Tater, and some Olive Oil. That's almost a meal right there. Before you, I had never met a Gardenia, after you I will probably never meet a Smalls. I don't remember who gave you the name Smalls, but I'm pretty sure I know why. Outside of the obvious, I'm not sure there's anything small about you.

When we met your first year I was not sure what kind of person you were. You were quiet and unassuming. Little did I know that humor, sarcasm, talent, and strength would define you? When we interviewed you for polo you said the superhero you wanted to be was spinach because spinach has E coli and E coli is going to take over the world. And you said it with such a straight face that I had to stop and process it. I mean seriously, who thinks about that?

The first time I saw you do a pushup, I was intimidated. You could do a pushup better than me. From that day forward you had another name "Personal Trainer". Another time you told me you might be a little late to practice, I asked why. Then you flexed and said, "I have to register these guns with the police department."

When you weren't a part of the program last year I was disappointed, partly because you worked hard and had talent, but mostly because you were fun to be around.

Your talent is not confined to the pool. I learned that this year after you won an award because of your artistic ability. When I asked you about it you just smiled and said "I like to draw." In addition, your strength is not confined to the pool. The strength you have demonstrated in dealing with the events of your family inspires me and should inspire all of us.

I will understand if, after high school, you choose to go by your given name. I hope you will also understand that you will always be Smalls to me. For it is in that name that so many fond memories will come back to me.

fleen

❖ The Headlights ❖
Ashley R

Headlights can be blinding. Many of us view a situation and think we have it all figured out. We can do it better than those currently in the process. Others just recognize who and where they are and simply do their very best.

Some people begin high school with the idea that they are going to mature and spread their wings come what may. Others simply enjoy high school while eagerly awaiting that next exciting step in life. On both accounts, I believe you to be more like the latter. That spotlight that many seek, as if validating some right of passage, is often frustrating, unfulfilling, and tiresome. Over the last four years your headlights have been on low beam.

I noticed the moment we met that you cared about what you did. Whether it had to do with people, school, or athletics, you cared. I wouldn't call that the average freshman trait. To call that normal in a freshman would be like saying your mom loves Hannah Montana. I mean she might, but who knew?

You have a way of separating yourself while being completely connected, enjoying the moment, yet not being consumed by it, and celebrating every positive thing that happens to you while not letting it define you. Your headlights have been on low beam.

You have worked hard to represent me, this program, your parents, and yourself in the best light possible yet many haven't realized just how much. You haven't let yourself get caught up in the all overwhelming drama that is high school. It's almost like you were ready for the next phase of your life before the next phase was ready for you. Your headlights have been on low beam.

There is so much I will remember and miss about you. I will miss your reliability. I will miss your smile. I will miss how you grew to be a leader both vocally, but more importantly by example. I will miss watching food fly out of your mouth while you talk. I will miss the times you accidentally called me dad. I will miss telling you to put on more clothing. And I will miss your crazy leg.

Finally as you go on from here, like a car driving off in the distance with its lights full of clarity, yet only on low beam, I will simply miss you.

fleen

Chapter Ten

2010

Dear Friend,

Imagine the feeling you get when you find a $20 bill in your coat pocket, you win a raffle at school, you discover your tax return is bigger than you thought, or your lost wallet is returned to you intact. Now multiply that feeling times ten and you can begin to understand what I feel at the end of every season. I get to see the joy on a kid's face when they are as excited to show me an improved grade as they are to get a best time. I get to see an athlete suffer through difficult practices then witness the fruits of their labor at CIF. I get to watch the freshman, who knew nothing about swim, go through the process of choosing which college they will continue their *swimming career. At the end of each season, I find $20 in every pocket of every coat I own.*

The first $20 I found was having the largest team I have ever had. We started with the biggest group ever in February. I honestly have no idea where these kids came from. I know two came from other schools and were shocked to discover how fun it was to swim at Cathedral City. Yeah, practices were hard, but the fun outweighed any temporary discomfort.

I found a $20 attached to almost every JV swimmer at some point during the season. To see them so excited about dropping time, being chosen swimmer of the week, having a pie thrown in their face, or singing in front of the team to get their forgotten equipment back. I was becoming richer by the day. I watched a freshman named Erika first learn how to swim, then learn fly, then swim fly in a Varsity meet, then become the 10th fastest Flyer at DVL. I watched another quiet freshman named Maria meet many new friends and come to love a sport she probably never thought she'd ever try. I listened to a foreign exchange student from France, who had never swum before, talk about how she was going to find a club to swim with when she returned home in June. I listened to another new swimmer named Maritza compliment me by calling me a "handsome individual." What athlete calls the coach who often inflicts pain on their body on a daily basis a "handsome individual?"

I also found a $20 attached to every Varsity girl. I watched another freshman named Camille suffer through a shoulder injury, when all she could do was kick for weeks, then swim best times as part of a 7th place 200 Free Relay and 11th Place 400 Free Relay at CIF. I saw Dani, one of my best senior polo players make a last minute decision to swim, then swim faster than she ever has before and for the first time make two individual time cuts for CIF. I also witnessed something I have never seen before in my 18 years of coaching. I watched all season as a first year junior named Christina dropped time meet after meet. Then set a class record in the 100 back and place 12th in the 50 Free and 13th in the 100 Back at CIF. Then split a 24.97 in the 200 Free Relay on the biggest stage at CIF. That is like finding a $100 bill in your pocket.

I also found $20 bills attached to each of the Varsity boys. I witnessed a senior named Aaron, who was dismissed from the team as a junior, come back and be an important part of two CIF qualifying relays. I watched a freshman named Austin surprise *all of us at seasons end by breaking 1:00 in his 100 free and swimming the 8th fastest backstroke at DVL. I watched a 2nd year swimmer named Claudio finally break 1:00 in his 100 Free then place 6th in the 500 Free at DVL and immediately begin talking about qualifying in that event for CIF next year. I watched as another 2nd year swimmer named Arquin, A.K.A. Manpedo, swim the 100 Fly at DVL Finals. Arquin was almost dismissed from the team his first year because he kept stopping and walking on the bottom of the pool during practice.*

I found $20 in the faces of all the athletes who were able to spend a week in Denver training and experiencing many things for the first time. Things like plane rides, ice skating, inner tubing in the snow, altitude, and major college campuses.

As you can see, I have become quite rich this year. As a teacher and coach, it is clear I did not choose my career path because of the pay. As you can also see, I become immeasurably richer by the end of each season. Part of the reason is the faithful support of people like you. Thank you again for believing in the mission of swim at Cathedral City.

Swimmingly

❖ The Good Nature ❖
Aaron M

There are people out there who think I live and die for swim. That it is the most important thing I do, the thing I can't do without. Comically enough, they couldn't be more mistaken. While I enjoy coaching, I also enjoy many other parts of my life. This is what I believe you and I have in common. We enjoy life, we choose things we like to do, and while we may be serious, we don't take ourselves very seriously. You are, as they say, good-natured.

I have seen you at times be incredibly understanding of people on the team. You'll encourage them, counsel them, even joke with them to make them feel better. You have a knack for the theatrical that is contagious. I don't know of many people who can sing verse, chorus, and background harmonies of Bohemian Rhapsody all at once. I used to think it was difficult for you to be in front of the team singing, but then I learned it was like oxygen for you. You play it off like you are uncomfortable then sing a classic Beatles song without missing a beat.

You also have developed a quiet maturity about you. It is difficult for athletes to come back after being dismissed from the team. Yet here you were without hesitation ready to face me and your senior year. I saw a renewed sense of commitment and work ethic from you this year that was very refreshing. You worked hard and really cared about improving. I was glad you were able to taste CIF again. It is a special place to be in the middle of May and your talent and dedication took you there.

I am glad you chose to swim this year. My teams need people like you. People that are talented, comical, devoted, and most of all good-natured.

fleen

❖ The Migration ❖
Amber S

Many things migrate. Most out of necessity. The idea of moving is never easy. Just ask anyone who has moved to a new job or a new house. It can be problematic and stressful. Yet somewhere in the middle of all the turmoil and uncertainty, sometimes things exist that keep us sane, content, and even happy. I hope swim was that for you.

I know there was some familiarity for you in that you had been part of the swim team at your previous high school. The fact that we swam against your team was even more ironic. Like birds flying south for the winter, there were certainly some things both schools you swam for had in common, but in many other ways, they were like night and day.

I am so happy you decided to be a part of our team. Your experience aside, it was fun to see you enjoy people, goofiness, and our silly traditions. I'm glad that you saw and experienced that we are more than a bunch of high school kids who are part of a team. You discovered that we are not about ability or popularity or gender or hairstyle, we are about substance, accountability, fun, and memories.

Thank you for jumping in feet first and involving yourself in such a positive way. Thank you for caring about your schoolwork. Thank you for working hard to improve yourself in spite of the things that tried to derail your season. Thank you for leaving your equipment behind and entertaining us. Thank <u>you</u> most of all for making <u>us</u> all feel welcome.

fleen

❖ **The Old Underwear** ❖
Cecelia T

Many of us have that old special thing we just can't part with. An old bag, a pair of jeans, that special pair of underwear with unique ventilation. We just don't want to let it go. Somehow I think that is what swim has been for you. Something you just can't live without. I too have those things I want to desperately keep. So I understand what swim means to you.

When you moved I remember your biggest concern was whether you could still swim for us. I knew the answer, but I also knew you would find a way to make it happen, and you did. You combined your passion for digital arts with your passion to swim and here you are today. That probably says more about you than anything.

To me, one of your greatest strengths is your ability to stretch yourself. You have a knack for having an interest and pursuing it, even if at first it does not come easy. You have a mind that is incredibly talented and creative. I think it drives you. I have seen it over and over in many people. This idea that passion drives purpose. Now I see it in you.

I have seen you at your most confident and I have seen you at your most insecure. Whether in front of a computer designing an amazing photo layout or in front of your team singing The Kooks, you do not back down.

I appreciate your desire to be a part of swim. While I know at times it has not been easy, I know you did whatever you could to not let it go. It is this quality that will make you an incredibly successful student in the future. I look forward to your return visits to the desert to tell me about the things you have learned and how you have stretched yourself even further. Because I know you will take with you, those special things you have learned while you were here. Those things you just don't want to let go of.

fleen

❖ **The New Girl** ❖
Dani S

When an athlete spends four years with me, they become a person I feel I've known forever. You on the other hand are someone I feel I just met. And the sad part is now you are leaving. It's not that I don't remember your first three years, I clearly do, it's that I'm not sure I appreciated the person you were during that time. You entered high school at a time when you and many other girls were tremendous people with smarts, personality, and incredible quirkiness.

You, like the others, didn't have a background in aquatics yet there you were improving like crazy. I could see it and was ecstatic for you, but I'm not sure I understood what aquatics meant to you, how important it was for you. You were a part of a very successful time for the girls in both swim and polo, yet here I was focusing sometimes on what you weren't doing rather than what you were. For this I am sorry.

And now you are leaving.

I now look back and remember things about you with ease. The skinny girl who made such a big improvement between her freshman and sophomore year. The smart, forgetful girl who would leave her homework, and many many other things behind. The incredibly artistic girl inside the spastic one. The girl who fell in love with water polo, the one who will play in college, the same one who almost gave it up. The 60's child who beats to her own drum, the one no one else can hear. The girl I could always count on to leave something behind, what Indie song would she sing next?

And now you are leaving.

While I am sad you are leaving, I am equally excited about your future. You have created it and its potential is limitless. We share a few things in common, but for the most part you and I aren't much alike. And now that I feel like I know you, the new girl, you are leaving. I will miss you Dani S.

Fleen

❖ The Unraveling ❖
Delilah A

They say that you can always count on change. Things just change. Whether we want them to or not, things in our lives have a way of changing. While at times we would prefer they not change, for some reason they do anyway. Even when we feel uncomfortable in the midst of change, looking back, we are often glad for the experience. That change, that growth, that unraveling is what I am happy to have seen in you over the past two years.

As is usually the case, I really don't know why people choose to swim. It honestly doesn't really matter. I enjoy the fact that anybody who really buys into our system, ultimately unravels...in a good way. They learn about themselves in ways they can't anticipate.

To say you were quiet and kept to yourself would be an understatement. The moon is also quiet and keeps to itself. I would take attendance and some days miss you because you were so stealth. But for some reason, I could always talk to you. You always had meaningful things to say, not trivial high school drama speak.

You continued to unravel even more this year. You learned and raced fly even though you probably didn't enjoy it that much... kind of like eating your vegetables. You interacted with more people and became an encourager to many. You listened intently and because you did I could see your confidence grow. One day I encouraged you to sing at the school's Coffee House. I was so thrilled later that night to receive a text that said "I did it...I sang!" It was then that I knew that your amazing creative side was also unraveling.

You are such a talented person in many ways. With your unraveling has come confidence. This confidence is a seed that will spark the growth of your bright future, you're very, very bright future.

fleen

❖ The Finish ❖
Kim S

When you sit down and think about it, everything we do generally has a beginning and an end. We wake up each day, do what we have to do, then the day comes to an end. We start a class and finish a class. We do the same with practice each day. Each day we start and finish hundreds of things. What separates us then is probably the degree to which we finish. What is incredible about you is not so much how you have started, but how you have finished.

Most people live their lives knowing how things they begin are going to finish. Life, for them, is easier this way. Your high school experience has been full of things you have started that you probably weren't sure how they were going to end. I have such admiration for people like this, for people like you.

Whether it was the classes you chose, the activities you became involved with, or the sports that became such a large part of your life, you have consistently chosen to not know the finish. Because of this you have become the incredible woman you are today.

You used to be a breaststroker, now you're a flyer and IM'er. You used to play 2 meters in polo, now you're an All-CIF goalie. You used to take CP classes, now you're one of the top students in school. You have chosen a path that has stretched you, molded you, and taught you that nothing is beyond your reach.

I firmly believe that when we give of ourselves, we get more than we bargained for in return. Thank you for all that you have given this program and me over the last four years. Because you have given so much, because you have consistently chosen roads you could not see the end of, your finish lines will be paved in gold.

fleen

❖ **The Name** ❖
Melanie H

I think your last name will be with me forever. My introduction to the name started with your sister, next in line was actually your dad, then you came along. As has been the case with every (insert last name) before you, you have been dedicated, a conscientious learner, and a quality individual. It will be odd to not see that name on my roster next year.

I remember you trying to find your way your freshman year. Once again, the last name made it easier, as many knew of it already. The transition was an easy one and you fit in nicely.

Your sophomore year was a breakthrough in many ways. You would qualify for CIF for the first time and drop time in each event you swam. The stage didn't seem to make you nervous at all. If anything, it energized you. You also seemed at home in Boston, even if you were literally stumbling your way everywhere.

After working hard to find your groove your junior year, you once again had great results at CIF. You have such a fluid stroke that is a joy to watch.

While your senior year might not have gone as well as you would have liked, I think you learned many things. It is my belief that we learn many lessons in success and disappointment. Lessons like taking nothing for granted, that achieving goals is a minute by minute process, and that the journey is almost more important than the destination.

I look forward to hearing about the journeys you will encounter while in college, the sacrifices you will make to reach your destinations, and the smile on your face as you tell me about each one.

fleen

❖ **The Impression** ❖
Ryley B

It is not easy to write certain letters. Some letters I think about long before I write them.

I often struggle with how to put the right words on paper. Words that try to demonstrate how important some people have been to the program, to the team, and to me. On one hand, I hope you know how difficult it was for me to write this for you. On the other hand, I hope you realize how proud I am of you, and how excited I am to see you move on.

I feel like I've known you forever. My introduction to you was many years ago as a middle school student. You were such an enthusiastic runner. Picking up the cards after each race with a smile and a giddy up. After a while, that wasn't enough. I heard some cheering at the end of the pool during one meet and in the middle of my team was Ryley teaching everyone a new move. I knew then and there I was going to enjoy having you on the team in the future.

You did not disappoint. Your unbridled enthusiasm was contagious, even if it was covered by a cheer uniform. You have this infectious way of becoming part of something positive. Whether in school or swim, it didn't matter. You saw the uniqueness of our swim team when you arrived and you believed in the concepts being taught. To say you were a believer is an understatement. You have probably given more to this program than this program has given to you. For that, I can't thank you enough.

You represent everything this team is about. If someone wanted to know what kind of team we were, I would tell them to just watch you. Watch how you encourage, how you work, how you lead, how you dance, how you laugh and smile, how you have no shame, and how you have the most incredible spirit.

I hope these past four years have been as much fun for you as they have been for me. Being the P.E. Major that I am, I do not have the words to tell you how much I will miss you. What I do know is you have left an impression I won't soon forget. With that will be many, many stories that will keep those who come after you inspired and laughing.

fleen

❖ **The Little Things** ❖
Veronica G

often have discussions with people about my favorite moments in swim. Many are surprised when I share with them an experience that is not centered around my best swimmer. They may know about the success of the program, but what they don't always know is the story about the athlete who doesn't always finish first. I take pride in giving everyone who wants to dedicate themselves to the core values of swim an opportunity to be a part of my team. That is why I am so grateful for you.

You have positively represented everything that is good about swimming at Cathedral City. I can honestly say you have never disappointed me. You have listened and you have learned. You have committed yourself academically and athletically without reservation. You are kind, giving, dedicated, and hardworking. There aren't many athletes who see a need and selflessly respond to it without being asked. This is you. I have seen you do it over and over for the last four years. What is more important is that others have also seen you do it.

I was so impressed by the things you did and sacrificed in order to come on the spring break trip this year. While others might have waited for that big chunk of money to arrive to pay for the trip, you slowly earned your way, little by little.

Even though you didn't feel well all week I was so happy to see you enjoy yourself. Whether it was watching you bowl, ice skate, play video games, go tubing, or eat cookies off your forehead, I will never forget Lil Wayne.

In a time when many are selfish, I thank you for being selfless. When others were looking for excuses, I thank you for starting with solutions. In moments of aimlessness, I thank you for being the beacon of light that showed direction.

Thank you for the little things you have done to make a big difference.

fleen

Chapter Eleven

2011

Dear Friend

I am fortunate enough to be able to spend each summer teaching English in Switzerland to kids from all over the globe. It is something I have done for many years and each year that I am able to return, I feel very lucky for the opportunity. I love seeing kids excited about learning a new language. They are always so eager. When I step off the plane I feel at home. I feel comfortable as if I'm entering another room in my house. I take a deep breath and look forward to beginning another summer of incredible experiences.

In many ways, this is how I feel about the opportunity to coach swimming at Cathedral City.

Each year I feel grateful for the chance to teach swimming. I'm excited, it feels very comfortable when the season begins, and I am eager to take kids from point A to point B.

While I have done this for 19 years, I am still thrilled to meet new kids, see familiar faces, and write a new chapter in the book that is Cathedral City Swim.

<u>Chapter One</u> begins with 70 kids deciding they want to try swimming. Something must have been in the water. I have never seen that many kids at the start of a season. Surprisingly, very few quit those first weeks. Since I do not cut anyone, everyone is welcome and the task of teaching them the ropes soon begins. Those first four weeks required a lot of work as the levels of ability were all over the place. I must say it was pretty fun watching them improve from day to day.

<u>Chapter Two</u> starts with our first meet. The energy and enthusiasm were so high that day. Unfortunately, so were the number of avoidable mistakes, and each team narrowly lost. While disappointed, that they couldn't enjoy the taste of victory, I was more than pleased as I left the deck.

<u>Chapter Three</u> begins very early in the morning as the team loads into cars to drive to LAX. The

destination is Honolulu, Hawaii for the team's annual spring break training trip. The tired eyes soon gave way to smiling faces as they stepped off the plane into a tropical paradise. The week was full of sightseeing, training, and laughter. Trips to Diamond Head, Pearl Harbor, the North Shore, and Hanauma Bay won't soon be forgotten. At the Luau watching the ENTIRE team get on stage to learn the traditional dance was amazing. That moment was soon topped by one happy senior girl who was chosen to dance alone with one of the performers in front of 700 people. I think she still has a smile on her face.

Chapter Four is a blur. The weeks pass quickly, as all of the teams are getting better and better and the season comes to a close. The JV and Varsity Girls teams would finish 8-4 while the Varsity Boys would set a new school record for wins, finishing at 9-3. While the girls were a mix of talent, the boys were the epitome of a team. From top to bottom the boys were solid and the new swimmers turned heads throughout the season with their incredible performances.

Chapter Five is a mix of emotions. The excitement of CIF was tempered with the league moving from Division III to Division II. The tough time standards made it difficult to qualify swimmers.

Had we been in Division III again, both the girls and boys would have qualified multiple athletes and relays. In reality, only one girl would qualify in only one event. But boy did she race well as she would finish 10th in her event with a best time and school record. The perfect ending as she prepares for the next chapter of her swimming career at San Jose State next Fall.

Chapter Six. This final chapter of 2011 is ending bittersweet as always. Not being able to see the kids on a daily basis anymore is always hard. They in turn are suddenly going from 100 miles an hour with the rigorous swim schedule to 10 miles an hour and too much free time. What will not be forgotten by anyone, athlete or coach is the tremendous memory-filled journey they have taken the last 3 months.

Credits. I'm so grateful to have former athletes such as Roz M, Gaby S, and Jenny R on staff to teach and encourage. I am appreciative of an administration that sees and appreciates the values and principles I try to teach my athletes. Finally, I am thankful for the generous financial support of our local community, many of who have stood with us for years.

As this year comes to a close I look forward to next year and the new chapters that will be written in the book that is Cathedral City Swim.

Swimmingly

❖ **The Little Things** ❖
Arquin A

When I look back at my years as a swim coach I feel blessed. I feel so lucky to make 37 cents an hour to teach kids how to swim and have fun. I have so many memories and stories to draw back upon. Stories of humor, inspiration, resolve, character, and grit. I will have many athletes who remind me of some of those qualities, but only a select few who represent all of them. Arquin A, you are one of those select few.

Your first days are still ingrained in my subconscious. After the first few days, it was "who are those people walking on the bottom of the pool?" After the first few weeks, it was "who is that guy still walking on the bottom of the pool? If he doesn't stop I'm not sure we can keep him." "Threaten him with bodily harm," I told my other coaches. "Maybe that will work."

Well, something clicked and you finally started swimming or doing something like swimming. It seemed more like you were boxing with the water, and you were losing. As coaches, we saw improvement, but I'm not sure I've seen anyone work harder and go nowhere.

Your second year, we wanted to try and get you a choice stroke. For some reason, you decided it needed to be fly… or something like fly. You worked hard, but well, you know the rest. The second meet, we gave you the fly and 1:40.51 later we were all so proud of you. The fact that you did it at DVL just topped off an amazing year for you.

This year you decided (or maybe I did) that IM… or something like IM was your next challenge. You were simply incredible. You have done so many things in and out of the pool that has made us all say, "did he just do that?" Beating a teammate in the breaststroke this year… twice, only added to the list of awe-inspiring things you have done over the last three years.

Rest assured, I will tell many stories about your swimming, your confusing looks, your roshambo skills, and your mind-boggling accomplishments. I gave the newspaper your name one time and the reporter said, "Arquin is a unique name, I've never heard it before." I smiled and simply said, "You have no idea how unique."

fleen

❖ **The Rare Breed** ❖
Kacey R

I hate to say it, but in high school we would not have gotten along at all. You were the kind of person I couldn't understand. I would think "how can that guy be so smart?" I had to work hard to be average. "And how can he be so smart and nice? Figures, he has to be funny too?" Well, I'm just glad I'm not in high school anymore and can appreciate all that you have managed to achieve these last four years.

You are definitely a rare breed. You chose a demanding academic schedule full of AP classes and a rigorous athletic schedule as well. After all, everyone knows water polo and swim are like the AP classes of sports. I guess that figures.

Like past four year athletes who were also Valedictorians, you are not defined by your academic accomplishments. You will be remembered for many other things as well.

You will be remembered by your devilish look we all recognized immediately as "DAMIEN." I'll admit, it was funny to the point that many people, myself included, wondered if you had an alien side. A side we all agreed we shouldn't mess with, just in case it were true.

You have a way of looking really good in make-up. Whether dressed in clothes that you, um, wear with make-up or buried in the sand with make-up, it kind of worked for you.

Then there is that Ninja Turtle shell thing you had going on. I'll admit I didn't realize you had to wear so much. First time I saw it I just thought it was related to the alien Damien thing and I never even dared about asking you about it.

You are definitely a rare breed. I appreciate all you have done to keep yourself focused while keeping the swim team traditions alive. Thank you for simply being a great person.

fleen

❖ **The Life Coach** ❖
Max B

As a teacher I hear many things about many people. To be fair, I try to reserve my opinion until I have first hand knowledge. I am in a position that requires patience, understanding, sympathy, and open-mindedness.

Four years ago I was told of an energetic young freshman who was doing well. For some reason every person had the same ending to their story. They all ended with "yeah...but." When I asked why the "yeah...but," the answer was always the same. "I can't understand him." "What do you mean?" I would say. They responded, "no seriously, I can't understand the words coming out of his mouth." I really thought they were just exaggerating, I mean how bad could it be? Then I met Max B. Everything they said was true.

The first time we met you spoke so fast I didn't understand two words. You must have thought something was wrong with <u>ME.</u> I just stood there and looked at the other kids and literally asked someone for a translation. It felt like my first year in Switzerland when I didn't know any German.

In the last four years, I have learned that you are more than a language enigma. You are a smart, talented, creative person with a huge heart for people. You have required me to learn to be more patient as I have tried to encourage and trust you with your schoolwork. You have taught me to be understanding of your views on a variety of levels. You have forged in me a new level of sympathy for people and the things they go through on a daily basis. Finally. you have reminded me that open-mindedness is a very valuable trait to have in life every single day.

As interesting as you have made my coaching career over the last four years. I would not trade a moment of anything. There are few things you can count on in life. Change is one of them. Thank you for teaching me four valuable lessons and for changing my life for the better.

fleen

❖ **The Dichotomy** ❖
Nadia L

I've been around high school students for far too long. Kind of like the heat of the desert, everywhere I go I can't escape it. What always intrigues me is the unique character that some students possess. It is not because they are brilliant or athletic or charismatic. It is not because they come from money or fame. It is certainly not because they have misrepresented themselves to the top. The answer lies in its simplicity. They are true to themselves.

You, Nadia L are true to yourself. The truth of your character lies in the dichotomy of what you are. You are not the top of your class, but you are extremely intelligent. You think more than the average student which is probably why high school seems boring to you at times. You are not always the big talker, but you have a special way of making me want to have conversations with you. My favorite are the ones where we don't agree on something. You are so insightful that I disagree sometimes just to watch you keep thinking. You've probably never realized this. I think it's part of your innocence. For example, seriously, how can anyone not like Lava Cakes?

The day you told me you weren't going to swim this year, I was very sad. It wasn't because of your talent, it was simply because I knew I would miss having you around. Then the day you changed your mind was one of the best days of swim for me.

You have an infectious smile, you have a witty charm, you have a genuine character, and you have a charismatic simplicity that few your age possess.

While high school has given you much, the next chapter of your life will give you even more. Being accepted to the most unique UC school in California is no surprise to me. For I believe that by choosing you, they have chosen the person I think is most true to themselves.

I will miss you when you leave, but I am happy for having had the chance to know you and the opportunity to know a person true to themselves.

fleen

❖ The Road Ahead ❖
Sam M

We take many paths in life. Some of those paths are very familiar to us. It is usually because we have taken that path before or it is easy to find the way. But the easy way is just that, it is easy. I remember your first go around at swim. It was not easy. There were bumps in the road and only you know how to describe your experience.

Fast forward to this year, your senior year. When you decided to swim I was thrilled as I knew you had talent. What I didn't know was how much of your first experience in swim you would bring to your second. What I did know was that you were a different person. While there are always parts of an experience that we don't always agree with or endorse, we must still support. It was at these moments during the season, and there were a few, that I knew you were different. That I knew you had changed.

Working hard and being committed to something is an incredibly important asset to a person's future. While we don't always know what lies at the end of that commitment, we know the journey to get there is worth it and can be surprising.

At DVL we spoke about the challenge before you. You were the top seed, but 2 guys were literally nipping at your toes. A bad start, a bad turn, too much excitement, and everything you wanted could disappear in an instant. Not only did you rise to the occasion you swam faster than you had all year.

When your best was required, you simply answered the call without wavering. It is this attitude that will be your guide as you move on from here. For now you, know the path is not always easy to see, but moving with conviction is like a beacon in the night.

fleen

❖ The Metamorphosis ❖
Sandra B

One of the things I like most about coaching are the people and their metamorphoses. Not to get all sciency or anything, but to me, the word signifies incredible change. The word literally means a transformation. The thing about metamorphosis for me is that it is a two-way street. I have opened up a new world of change for you, but you have also done that for me.

I remember you last year as someone looking for fun and not just waiting for the fun to "happen" to them. You somehow understood what the foundation for swim at Cathedral City was all about. You work hard, have fun, then pass it on.

In addition, you were a quick learner. As the season ended a year ago I remember how excited you were for swim to start the next year. Your enthusiasm was contagious as I'm sure you wanted to make the most of your senior year.

I can only imagine the change in you, had you been able to swim all four years. I can't even fathom how much more experience you would have gained, how much more fun you would have had, how many more friends you would have made, and how positive of an influence you would have infected the team with.

I am both happy and sad. I am grateful you chose to swim and thankful you enjoyed it so much. I am happy you and I both experienced this metamorphosis together. I am sad it only lasted two years.

I can still see you laughing and singing. I can still see you trying to do fly and breast, but somehow you managed to transform the two together to make a stroke I have never seen before. I can still see you, with a smile, challenging me daily to "fight you".

I am thankful that in two short years we have both gone through a metamorphosis.

fleen

Chapter Twelve

2012

Dear Friend

Christmas in May? Someone must have gotten a hold of some ancient calendar from some far gone society. We all know that the multitude of gifts that accompany the Christmas tradition is in the dead of winter, not the heat of May. Or is it? As coach of the swim team at Cathedral City, I have come to look forward to the stories of May as much as I have the joys of December. In that respect, I am very lucky. For it is in May that I have the pleasure of finally seeing the many gifts that have been three months in the making.

The first gift I received wasthe 75 new faces I saw try out for a team with no pool and no feeder program. What kind of kid wants to be on a swim team at that kind of school anyway? Apparently a lot of kids. It was by far the biggest team in school history.

The next gift took a while to open. Sophomore Tristan P did well as a freshman, but nothing to write home about. Put it this way, she had never swum before and could really only do freestyle. She had never swum anything but freestyle in a meet… ever. This year was certainly different. Let's just say she had to change her goal times for the season almost weekly. At DVL league finals she would end up 4th in the 100 Free and 5th in the 100 Back.

A large gift, the boys team, was challenging to open at times. Instead of returning what I thought would be an entire team, only a fraction of the boys' returned to swim. Yet there they were, a season record of 6-6 with five DVL titles easily within reach. Watching new swimmers like Shayan E, Lance T, Mohammed Z, Chris C, Alex F, Conner E, Marco P, and Jeff P go through the ups and downs of learning was very gratifying. Each would surprise themselves by the end of the season.

One of the most difficult gifts to open was watching a handful of athletes chase CIF qualifying times. For the 2nd straight year, the Desert Valley

League was placed in Division II at CIF. The times required to qualify were much faster than Division III. While no one would ultimately qualify, it was exhilarating to see the efforts put forth by Camille K, Sam C, Creyton B, and a girls' relay team. They should be extremely proud, as I was, of the work they put in to reach that goal.

A unique gift arrived in the form of Lenny G. I came to learn that one of the reasons she decided to swim was to overcome a fear of the water. To be clear, that is usually not why most people join competitive swim teams. The first few weeks her best friends were the lane line, the wall, and the bottom of the pool. By the end of the season, you would not have recognized her. She swam many different events and after watching her dive you would have never thought she was ever afraid of the water.

Spring Break is like opening 50 gifts each day for a week. Picture 24 kids away from home in San Diego, at the beach every day, training 2x a day, eating like maniacs, with no fear of anything and no shame at all. While many coaches would never subject themselves to such hysteria on their spring break, I can't wait to create some of the best memories they will ever have. With most of it 'caught on tape', they will have stories for a lifetime. Some read amazing emotional poetry, some learned they could not bowl at all, some have tremendous fashion sense, and some learned they couldn't shoot the ocean if they were standing on the beach while playing laser tag. At the end of the week, team Vicious & Delicious won the team activity competition. There really is nothing like 30 people invading a small restaurant and making their presence felt... immediately. Bottom line; there was not one kid on that trip who didn't make the coaches laugh multiple times a day.

I could write ten pages about the other gifts the coaches received throughout the season. For me, a December Christmas is actually not so much about the gifts as it is about spending time with family. It's about spending time with people I care about. This is how I feel about my May Christmas. I am grateful for the chance to see kids discover, learn, and accomplish. I love opening all the surprising gifts each season, I love it when their eyes are as happy as mine over something they've done and I love the fact the biggest joys come from experiencing it all with people I truly care about. Thank you for continuing to support Cathedral City Swimming.

Swimmingly

❖ **The Tattoo** ❖
Creyton B

I don't think I'll ever be the tattoo kind of person. It's just not me. When I get old, that king's crown on my arm will probably look like a meadow full of dead wildebeests. I don't even like wildebeests when they're alive. Over the years a few swimmers have left their mark on me. You could even say they've left their tattoo. It's true, I think I have a tattoo of Creyton B. Oddly enough, as unique as the tattoo is, it keeps changing.

The first group of swimmers I ever had felt like they were in high school for 5 years. You, on the other hand, I feel like you have been on the team for 7 years. Maybe it's because I knew you before high school or maybe it's because the team has undergone so many changes over the years. Honestly, I think it's because you have also gone through so many changes.

Outside sources would probably disagree. If they look at you now they'd tend to think you haven't changed much at all. They would see your fierce competitive spirit, your extreme dedication, your intense loyalty, and your genuine inclusive nature and sense of self-confidence. Those are some incredible attributes. We should all be so lucky. I would agree that 7 years ago, those traits existed in you. I would also suggest that those are the same traits that have changed in you.

You are one of the unique few whose strengths I can also count as weaknesses. The remarkable qualities that could lead you to the top rung, could also be the ones that keep you off the first step. Because you have such an insatiable desire to live and leave your mark, I have no doubt that you will reach the top.

Please know this. I am confident you will leave a tattoo on many people in your lifetime. Even though the tattoo may change, those who wear it will wear it proudly. I am one of them.

fleen

❖ **The Soul** ❖
Elizabeth G

As an anatomy teacher I am very familiar with the structure of the human body. I can tell you exactly how each system works, the parts involved, and the issues that arise when something isn't working properly, but what I can't tell you is anything about the soul. I don't know what it looks like, I don't know how it functions, and I certainly couldn't explain why it is so important. When it comes to people I just know it's important to have one. You, Elizabeth Garcia, have become like the soul of my program. I may be able to take credit for many aspects of swim, but I can't take credit for the development of its soul. I can tell you that it is important to have one.

When you began as a freshman, I'm sure that becoming the soul of the team was not high on your list of goals. I'm guessing you were just focused on getting to the other side. Having had two older sisters in swim before you probably had a lot to do with you learning how important it is to enjoy the experience. Seeing them laughing, meeting new people, and bringing home stories about swim had to be intriguing.

As each year went by I could see you enjoy it more and more, the bus rides, the singing, the traditions, the practices (OK maybe not the practices). The laughter and unbridled silliness that seems to follow us could be seen in your soul. I would see external evidence every now and then, but mostly it was your infectious smile and caring spirit.

The swim program has always had a heart, but not always a soul. Athletes would come to learn about our traditions, but not always why we have them. You knew the why. Students have come to know why I stress academic accountability. They usually think it's about getting A's & B's, but you knew it was about actually learning something. Being kind, encouraging, and welcoming has always been a staple of the team. While some have had to learn how to do this, you on the other hand already seem to know. I believe it is because you have a tremendous soul.

This team will miss you when you go. More importantly, this team will miss your soul.

fleen

❖ **The Talent** ❖
Jeff P

Who is he? That fateful question often asked when you can't explain something or in your case someone. Who is Jeff P? One person will say "Jeff, he's that DVL Champion wrestler," another "oh yeah, he's that actor," still another "You mean Jeff the singer?" Someone even said

"I know Jeff, he's that tattooed skater with purple hair, right? I'm guessing they didn't really know you. Well, I would like to add one more; "Jeff the swimmer."

I must admit I really didn't know who you were. I think I remember seeing you in some school plays and someone said you played water polo your freshman year. Knowing you were a much needed guy for the team I was thrilled you decided to swim. Like most people who try swimming at the end of their high school experience, you were a little rough around the edges. I must say that I liked your effort, your willingness to learn, your commitment to the team, and your good-natured character. By the end of the season, it was clear that you were truly a swimmer.

What I also appreciated was your forgetfulness. In other programs you may get away with such uninspiring use of brain cells, but not in swim. Swim loves those who lose touch with reality. It makes for incredible moments that have nothing to do with water. As a swim coach, that is important to me.

The only thing that made these moments more memorable was when others athletes stole your equipment and gave it to me. Your reaction as you saw your equipment in my hands with my "yes it's true, you are going to sing again" face on, would soon become the highlight of my day.

Your performances (yes it was a performance and yes the plural tense is the correct tense) had everyone captivated. The girls, and even some of the guys, were clearly on the edge of tears during some of your best moments. Your ability to take us through a roller coaster of emotions was award-winning. All this while standing on a pool deck. Now that is talent.

I am sorry you won't be gracing us with your talents as a swimmer and performer. I will miss those times. I am confident though that these moments will only get better as you go on to display the talent that is Jeff P.

fleen

❖ **The Secret Weapon** ❖
Lacey W

The Avengers is one of the most popular movies out right now. Six superheroes, each with their own special talent. We should all be so lucky. What I'm wondering is why they didn't ask if you were available? I mean who wouldn't want "THE LACEY" fighting the criminal elements of the dark side? The innocent face with the deadly elbow. No one would see it coming. What many don't know is that is not your only secret weapon.

The Elbow. Everyone and I mean everyone, knows your elbows are dangerous with a mind of their own. And they don't just nudge, damage, or bruise, they penetrate, slice, and maim. Most of your victims were unwitting teammates. Unfortunately one of those victims was often your sister.

The Brainieator. Those cells inside your head are lethal. Not many could handle the demands of swim, water polo, school, and me. Yet there you were working hard to be the best you could be in every area.

The Dedicator. You have been one of the most committed student-athletes this program has ever known. I can't remember you ever using any of the hundreds of lame excuses I get for missing a practice. What I can remember is you not wanting to miss a practice, practicing sick, or me having to tell you you can't practice.

The Flexor. You're like a pufferfish. Small and diminutive one minute, looking extremely menacing the next. Sometimes you would just flex for no reason. But we all knew the real reason. Those guns were pointed at us with a simple message "don't make me turn these on." Our smiles were usually enough for you to put them away.

Your final secret weapon, a pure heart. We should all have such a weapon. You are true to yourself. You know your strengths and your limitations. You are fearful of nothing and eager to try anything. You embody integrity and understand that things worth having are worthy of sacrifice. All I can say is, world watch out, here comes "THE LACEY!"

fleen

The Change
Lorena C

One of the things I treasure most about coaching is change. Sometimes that change is not good, but most of the time it is priceless. I can't tell you how many times I have seen it.

Every time I see it, I want more. Nobody provides more change than a new swimmer. One of life's mysteries is why a senior would want to join swim at Cathedral City. Is it because they practice harder and more often than most schools, is it because everyone is treated as equals regardless of experience, or is it because they are held academically accountable? Maybe the answer is as simple as, they want change.

As a coach, I am happy to offer people change. You must have realized this early as you were like a caterpillar becoming a butterfly. I remember the early days. I could see you struggling at the beginning as you were learning the strokes and how to practice. I could see you reach out to others on the team. I could see you feeling more and more comfortable each day. I could see the change.

I was stopped by a teacher in the office one day. I have known him a long time and he is a fan of the swim program. After some small talk he asked me "how is Lorena doing in swim?" Before I could even answer he said "because she seems to really love it." He then went on to explain how before swim you were pretty quiet and reserved in class. Since swim started he said you have become more confident, energetic, and assertive. He seemed so genuinely happy about the changes in you since you joined the team.

I couldn't have been more proud of you at that moment. I realized it didn't matter why you decided to swim. I'm just glad you did.

fleen

❖ **The Storyteller** ❖
Lorrie T

I think we all agree that not many people tell a story like Lorrie T. It's not so much the content or delivery, it's just that we don't seem to ever know when you are finished. Your stories are often followed by that awkward silence or an "um…yeah." The rest of us don't know whether we can say something or if there is more story to come. Your junior year I even suggested you say "I'm done" at the end of your stories so that we knew we had the green light to speak. For most of us, that's the point. In life, we never know when we are done telling our stories. All we know is there will be another one.

Your story, like most peoples, didn't always

follow a clear-cut pattern. While you may have been uncertain at times about which direction to go, I believe you did your best to make the best choice. I am thankful for the effort you put into my teams and the improvement you made as an athlete. I am very pleased that you made school a priority and worked hard to do your best with a busy schedule. I applaud your dedication to the HEAL Academy and the leadership roles you filled the past few years.

<u>So many changes in so few years</u> could be the battle cry for the high school experience. With so many forks in the road, you are asked to constantly rewrite your story. While many stories have a happy ending, some don't always end the way you want. Ultimately that is the beauty.

Mice love cheese. Put them in a maze and they will find it. Change nothing for a month and they will get fat. Move the cheese and they will either keep following the same path hoping the cheese returns or take a different path looking for new cheese. As you go on from here, two things will be certain, one, someone at some point will move your cheese, and two, there will always be more cheese waiting for you somewhere.

fleen

❖ **The Difference** ❖
Maritza M

When you spend a lot of time with people you sometimes are not aware of the subtle changes that occur. On the other hand, when I don't see people for a while or when I'm in a new environment I tend to notice things more. One of the things I cherish as an educator and coach is to see change, growth, and improvement. While some kids may only change in appearance over the course of high school, others are transformed in many ways. Transformation happens only in the company of openness.

When I look at you now, I see the difference.

Let's just say that when you first joined the team, a career in counseling was not in your future. Blunt, to the point, and impatient may have been some of your better qualities. Subtlety, restraint, and empathy were clearly words on some else's spelling test. If you barked without a bite, that person was considered a friend. Oddly enough, as a sophomore, you were a peer counselor.

When I look at you now, I see the difference.

At first it seemed hard for you to understand how and what I was trying to teach. At times you felt you were doing what I asked and I felt you weren't. I could see the frustration, but I could also see you trying. Others would see you questioning me and be surprised, I would welcome the questioning and look forward to the result.

When I look at you now I see the difference.

On the outside, we are very different, but on the inside, I think we are quite similar. You see I too have a dark side that people are fearful of, yet most wouldn't want it any other way. Like you I would do anything for those I care about. And like you, I will be honest to a fault.

I am going to miss you screaming at kids, I am going to miss you telling it straight, and I am going to miss you making freshmen wish they were back in 8th grade. Most of all I am going to miss the daily opportunity to see the difference.

fleen

❖ The Times like these ❖
Sam C

There is a Foo Fighter's song called "Times like these." I think your experience can be summed up in the lyrics to the chorus. <u>It's times like these you learn to live again. It's times like these you give and give again. It's times like these you learn to love again. It's times like these time and time again.</u> The lyrics have a serious tone to them, but as I relate the words to you they also show a lighter side.

The first line of the chorus makes me think about how much you have grown as a student, athlete, and person. I can remember many times how things may not have gone according to plan, yet there you were learning to live again. Never focusing on the past, just looking ahead at what was next.

To me, the second line epitomizes you. You were always doing your best to give. Once you understood the importance of traditions in the program, you were first in line to make sure they continued. Your forgetfulness may have had something to do with it. I'll never forget you telling me you wouldn't have to sing this year because you forget your equipment. After all, you sang every year, multiple times. Fate was not your friend, you sang twice the last week.

The third verse reminds me of how much you truly enjoyed being a part of the program. You were always a hard worker, a talented swimmer, comically forgetful, and a joy to have around. That's why it appeared you were always learning to love it all, over and over again every year.

The final verse will always make me think of you with a smile. I can still imagine your singing, your dancing ability, your unique form of common sense, your ability to enter a conversation then not know what was being discussed, and your kind nature. This and more is what I will remember, time and time again.

fleen

Chapter Thirteen

2013

Dear Friend,

Every year I'm reminded why I enjoy coaching. Eager learners, smiling faces, energetic kids, and wide-eyed newcomers are but a few of the reasons I continue to do this year after year. The 2013 version of Cathedral City Swimming, once again, reinforced why I love to coach. One of my favorite expressions is simple and couldn't have been more accurate to explain this year. 'It's about the journey, not the destination."

The journey began with over 80 swimmers piling into busses too small to carry them to practice. While that number would settle into the mid 60's by season's end, it did create some unusual situations. For the second year, the girls' team would field a second JV team. Last year it happened on occasion. This year, if the opposing team was willing, it happened every meet. Not just a handful, but a full 2nd level of JV girls. I seriously had to consider my policy of not cutting anyone. We didn't always have space on the bus, have enough equipment, or have enough money to cover expenses, but somehow we made it happen. I was thrilled to be able to offer them this journey.

For the second year in a row, we would have athletes work incredibly hard, yet come up just short of qualifying for CIF. Seniors Camille K and Kenny G would be two of the top swimmers in the DVL yet just miss out on qualifying at the DVL meet. As disappointing as it was for them, to hear them talk on the bus on the way home about how much they enjoyed their experiences as Cathedral City swimmers over the past four years was heartwarming. It is clear they enjoyed the journey.

Portland, Oregon was the destination for our annual spring break trip. As usual it was hard to see who enjoyed the trip more, the athletes or the chaperones. Everyone had smiles on their faces. The weather report all week leading up to the trip was cold and wet. When the team arrived, the days were partly to mostly sunny with only a few brief periods of rain to remind the team that they were indeed in Oregon. Green and beautiful highlighted each day. Planned trips to Multnomah Falls, downtown Portland, and the University of Portland were followed by many surprises for the week.

Surprise #1 was a trip to Mt Hood to go inner tubing. They had no idea where we were going. They just knew it was getting colder and whiter. The chaperones must have thought they were 17 again sliding down the mountain with huge smiles. The swimmers had a little trouble navigating the snow but never slowed down. Sliding, tubing, crashing, building snow sculptures, and snowball fights filled the afternoon.

Surprise #2 was a visit to the historic coastal town of Seaside. The Oregon coast is much different than the California coast. Sunny and brisk pretty much summed up the day, but it didn't stop a few courageous athletes from testing the chilly waters.

Surprise #3 was a trip to my hometown of Eugene. It was an all day adventure filled with visits to the University of Oregon football complex and bookstore, a tour of where I grew up and schools I attended, and a meet and greet with my parents and older brother. I think many of the swimmers were surprised I actually had a family. The day was capped off with a tour of the University of Oregon campus followed by our annual intrasquad meet, again on the campus of the U of O.

This year's journey was bittersweet. Having so many kids work so hard and not reach the goals they set for themselves was disappointing. Yet as the athletes and myself reflect back, our thoughts will quickly turn to the many memorable experiences that filled the season, the many new friends that were made, and the satisfaction of knowing that we all gave everything we had. 2013 was an amazing journey.

Thank you again for all you do to support the swim journey at Cathedral City.

Swimmingly

❖ **The Foundation** ❖
Camille K

Your high school experience has been a bit of a roller coaster. I feel like you have had an inordinate amount of highs and lows throughout… more than the average student/athlete. The fact that you have a tremendously strong foundation is one of the reasons why you have risen to the top.

You arrived with high expectations and quickly established yourself as a committed, hard-working athlete, and dedicated student. From the lows of not being able to train in Denver to the highs of a great experience at CIF, you persevered.

The next three years would present the challenges of completing a difficult class load, managing nagging injuries, and balancing a full load of activities while trying to lead young and inexperienced teams. While difficult at times, I believe your strong foundation kept you focused and motivated.

I have seen many sides of you over the last four years. From strong to weak, confident to uncertain, and untouchable to vulnerable. Through it all, I have always appreciated your steadfastness.

I am confident you will do well as you move on to college and beyond. I hope you continue to decipher between those traits that add to your foundation (yes, twerking is one of them) and those that might not.

Thank you, for giving all of yourself over the last four years. I can't think of a better foundation than the one you have created for yourself.

fleen

❖ **The Understanding** ❖
Danielle K

Not having a swim background makes me the perfect person to coach swim. I don't have swim baggage from my childhood, I don't know what it feels like to be yelled at by an irate coach with a stopwatch, and I don't know how it feels to do my best and be told it wasn't enough. That's what I think you and I have in common. We just focus on the process and on enjoying the moment.

There is so much to be thankful for when you are part of a team that works as hard as we do. I think you understand that. It is so refreshing to know that no other team has as much fun as we do. I know you understand that.

What I have always appreciated about you is how much you understand the team. While there were times you and I both know you probably didn't make the best choice, you still understood the team. In the good and the bad, you have always understood the team.

To understand that there is a system and to accept your fate within that system, is a tremendous asset to have. I hope you also understand that your efforts and commitment did not go unnoticed. I actually see you in a position not unlike mine, mentoring others in a situation that might be unfamiliar to you. I also see you being successful because above all, you understand what it takes.

fleen

❖ The Stages of Swim ❖
Emily R

Why does a senior try swimming for the first time? I could make an argument for many reasons, but it always seems to come down to the same one. P.E. credit. While I understand this, I also understand that they are in for the ride of their life. So here you are, the stages of new senior swimming.

<u>Stage one.</u> This is hard and I'm not as good as I thought I was. I mean, I take a shower everyday, sometimes I even take a bath. I 'swim' at my friends' backyard pool, but for some reason that was so much easier than this. There are so many people better than me. Is this something I really want to continue?

<u>Stage two.</u> I made it through the first month. I'm still not that great, but at least I have company. The people in my lane are just like me. I'm actually even better than some and I can even read the clock. The team is weird. They yell and scream a lot... just for fun. Even though it's my first year I'm treated like everyone else. One girl had to sing to get her equipment back. I'm never going to forget my equipment. I think I might stick with this.

<u>Stage three.</u> I'm actually getting faster. Coach said the clock never lies and he's right. My times are getting faster. I feel like a swimmer. I'm experiencing this strange dichotomy. I eat like a horse, but my clothes are too big for me now. I think I like swim.

<u>Stage four.</u> I can't believe this is over. I saw my time trials and can't believe I was ever that slow. I actually wish I left my equipment behind just

once. It would have been fun to be goofy. Why didn't I do this as a freshman?

fleen

❖ **The Exception** ❖
Erica G

As coaches, we often feel like we live in a bubble. I would have to say that this is true for me. I know my classroom and the students I teach, and I know the pool and the athletes I coach. Beyond that, I don't know where they go after practice any more than they know where I go after practice. I often have a newfound respect for athletes when I learn the 'where they go.' You are like many. I see you and appreciate your talent, your work ethic, and most importantly, your fun loving sense of humor. You could literally say with a big smile and genuine eyes that you were going to steal my car and sell the parts to earn enough money to become a locksmith just so you could break into my house and steal all of my furniture. I would just smile back, not knowing if you were serious, but also not stupid enough to doubt you.

You have to remember that you were an exception when you started swim. You weren't supposed to be around. To say that your grades were not good would be like saying Usher was an OK dancer. But then you explained to me why, and I understood. What I learned that day was 'where you go' after practice. I allowed you to swim and you responded with the biggest grade improvement of anyone on the team.

I was proud of you then and I am still very proud of you now. You have a special sincerity that I believe will be your guiding light as you move on to the next phase of your life. I have no doubt, that in the future, you will make many more people proud of you.

fleen

❖ The Statement ❖
Erika W

M any people are afraid to speak their mind, say what they feel, rock the boat. You, on the other hand, to me, are like a breath of fresh air. I don't know where you got it, but I love the fact that you don't hold back.

I will never forget the look that I affectionately came to identify as the IDC. I don't care. You would be faced with a question, statement, concern, or opinion and your expression, like a beacon in the night would speak volumes. The infinitely famous, yet expressionless, IDC. No words were ever necessary for you.

I remember the many times' teammates tried to pair you up with someone for a dance. They would describe in great detail how you would be perfect together. They would go so far as to choose your dress, describe the itinerary of the evening to the second, and joyously plan the epic relationship that would ensue as a result of their match-making ability. Your response was always Erika-ess. The IDC followed by a succinct 'No' or colorful 'he's dumb.' I love that about you. You know exactly who you are.

But what I will always remember about you is Portland. You were open, stepping out of your comfort zone, dare I say even goofy. You tried new things and while you may not have enjoyed everything, you eagerly tried it all. From food to activities, you stretched yourself.

I must admit, I was worried for you, in moving on to college, that you would be trapped in your

IDC. Now I have no doubt you will try, absorb, process, and stretch yourself as you move on from here. I bet you'll even end up on a reality TV show. OK, that might be asking for too much.

fleen

❖ **The Secret** ❖
Jacquline C

I t is no secret that I coach because I love it. I sometimes learn more and have more fun than my athletes do. I have the good fortune of being able to look back over years and remember athletes with incredible fondness. I can't imagine having someone try out only to find they can't be a part of the team. If that were the case, I think I would have missed out on some of the best memories of my coaching experience.

Watching you find your way through swim and water polo these past two years has been a joy to experience. I love the way you work in the pool and in the classroom. I love your sincere enthusiasm and your sarcastic nature. And, I love that you speak your mind at any moment.

Some examples. #1 You walk into my classroom in the morning to see what you'll swim that day. I see you process the events, slowly walk over to me, and with no hint of a smile say, "Fleen, why do you hate me?" #2 So as not to get bored with myself I sometimes say everything exceptionally loud or talk with a British, Australian, or Tanzanian accent to which you say with no hint of a smile, "Fleen, you are so strange." You always seem to start any conversation with me by saying "Fleen" first. I love that!

I was so happy to be able to share Portland with you. I was so worried when you thought at one point you wouldn't be able to go. You seemed to enjoy the week and all the activities so much.

Thank you for being such a positive part of the team. You represent the reason I want everyone to enjoy swim at Cathedral City.

Just to be clear: no I don't hate you and yes I am strange.

fleen

❖ **The Drummer** ❖
Jennifer W

'll get right to the point. We've all heard the expression 'beat to your own drum.' Well, that doesn't even begin to describe Jennifer W. You beat, bang, clang, thump, and kaboom to your own drum. That drum is so worn out it screams every time you hit it.

It began your freshman year when I gave you the name <u>two sock</u>. Let's just say I would be very poor if I had a nickel for every time I saw you wearing matching socks.

Your sophomore year you seemed to prefer the stage. When you found out you had to sing to get back forgotten equipment, I honestly think you left things behind on purpose. The problem came when you had to sing. They say you can tune a piano but, you can't tune a fish. Let's just say you were a tuna fish.

Your junior year there was widespread debate on whether you were human or animal. Most of the time human sounds came out of your mouth that most people could discern. Occasionally though, we would hear such an unrecognizable sound accompanied by the most Ffrankenstienian face that I often pondered on the origin of your DNA.

This year, two phrases will be forever etched in my brain. Both of which were heard over and over again, often at the most inappropriate of times. 'YOLO' and 'my husband Chris.'

I feel very confident in saying I have no clue what the future holds for you. But I feel very confident in saying that it will not be boring. I, for one, can't wait to find out.

fleen

❖ **The Select Few** ❖
Karina R

They say the hardest thing to do when you are starting to learn something is to just start. Sometimes it is not pretty, but hey you gotta start somewhere right? Babies try all the holes above their neck before they figure out that food tastes better when it's in their mouth. Beethoven probably made the hair on his parent's neck stand up when he first started playing the violin. Even Michael Phelps couldn't put his head in the water when he started swimming and floated on his back everywhere.

Then there was Karina. I have this vivid memory of you as a freshman trying out for water polo. It's the first time in the deep end. Everyone was moving back and forth and you couldn't move back or forth. You clung to the wall like grass clings to the earth. One day you let go of the earth. To your amazement and mine, you didn't sink... that much. You were 5 feet away from the wall and I remember asking you to come to the wall and you literally took 48 strokes, some underwater, to get there. We all thought that would be the end of it. The next day you came back, then again, again, and again. You wouldn't quit. To look at you now, no one would have thought you would have started like that. Now four years later, you have played polo and swam every year. You've even become a flyer and IM'er.

You are part of a small select few who have never said no, never backed down, never thought of quitting, and never stopped inspiring those around you. I can only imagine the impact you will have on those around you as you go on from here. You have learned so much these past four years, but I think we have learned even more from you.

fleen

❖ The Edge of Greatness ❖
Kenny G

Greatness is a word all of us would like associated with our name, like kind, hardworking, humble, and determined. Greatness conjures up a plethora of positive adjectives that most of us would be proud of. Many people are good, few are great. The ironic part is the jump from good to great is but a short leap of faith.

It's been fun watching you grow, literally and figuratively, from your freshman year. When you began you were like a newborn deer learning to walk, gawky and unsure, but full of potential that all could see. You're 1.11.13 100 free and 2.41.06 200 free weren't much to look at, at the time.

Your growth has not been limited to just your swimming ability. Your achievement in school and development as a team leader were also a bit shaky when you started. Finding your way in a new environment is a little like walking around in your house in the dark. You know the lay of the house, but with the lights off you have to trust that you remember how everything is laid out.

I believe the gap from good to great for you is more of a step than a jump. I hope that as you move forward from here you have the faith in yourself to see that greatness is in your future.

fleen

❖ **The Jump** ❖
Lenny G

They say stretching before exercise is good for you. As a Physical Education major, they said this to us all the time. So when I started coaching I would provide time for this. What I have since learned, and exercise physiologists agree with, is that easy exercise similar to the actual sport is better. You must have been an exercise physiologist in another life because you seemed to already understand this concept.

You see, one of the things I have learned about you is that you don't need to do some unrelated movement before you move. You just jump right in. I learned this when you joined wrestling, I learned when you joined swim, and I learned this as evidenced by your 4.0 GPA.

While swim might have seemed normal, wrestling was not. While CP classes might have seemed normal, AP & Honors classes were not. I would imagine that at some point all of these things were a struggle, but there you were, jumping right in. Who needs to stretch? I believe it speaks volumes about your effort, your willingness to try anything, and your character to never quit.

I can only imagine what your future will hold for you. I am fairly confident you will try many new things, each of which will continue to define who you are as a person. I am just glad you decided to jump into swim.

fleen

❖ **The Transformation** ❖
Maria M

When we are young our parents tell us many things, mostly things to protect us. To make sure we make the right choice. Things like, look both ways before you cross the street. Don't blow-dry your hair in the shower. And no matter how fast you want it, don't cook the egg in the microwave.

When you started swim I could see your hesitation and questioning nature. Not so much to be on the safe side, but more the pleasing side. You seemed a little unsure at the beginning. What is all this craziness going on around me? This was the hesitation side. Are these people for real? This was the questioning side.

As you have grown you have blossomed into this fun-loving, positive, zany, determined, comical, and committed athlete. Yours is the classic metamorphosis from freshman learner to senior leader. You represent everything this team is about. You never complained once. You always tried your best, and you did it without being asked and without reservation. I was so happy you had the chance to go to Portland. I don't think I ever saw you without a smile on your face the whole week.

I really hope you have enjoyed swim as much as I have enjoyed having you on the team. I am fully confident that the lessons you have learned will ensure your future success. I can't wait to hear all of your success stories.

fleen

❖ **The Home** ❖
Maria Elena A

One of the best gifts I can give my athletes is a home. You know that place where no one cares how you act or what you look like. Where no one cares if you swam well or not so well. Where no one cares if you dropped the ball or picked it up for someone else. This home is a place where you are not judged. It is a home where you are unconditionally accepted. You, Maria Elena, have found a home in swim. And I have photographic and video proof.

I discovered just how Emo you truly are when you sang for the team… multiple times. You even made me contemplate crying four tears in one eye once. This quiet and soft-spoken girl we all know suddenly found her stage singing in front of 50 over-chlorinated teenagers. Because you were at home, it was OK.

I also learned that you could bust a move. I saw the video in the van and personally, I think you were holding back a little. Some of the other girls even stopped dancing and thought with awe as they watched you shake it, "That girl's got groove!" Because you were at home, it was OK.

Then I found out about the hair. You had been holding out on me all of these years. Your straightener was working overtime. Your hair puts the wave in wavy, the fro in afro, and the bed in bedhead. I was so impressed that I didn't let you fix it or cover it in Portland. The world needed to see it. Funny thing is, I see it much more now. Because you are at home, it is OK.

I am happy you have found a home in swim. You will always have a home in swim. I can't wait to see a picture of you in college. And please, don't crop out the hair.

fleen

❖ The Text ❖
Tierney M

Let me just start by saying, I will miss you. I will miss your performances. I honestly think you are probably in the top five in how many times you had to sing for the team. And each time you didn't disappoint. I will miss telling you and hearing coaches tell you the same thing over and over and over again. I will miss your texts. From the season premiere of American Idol to the season finale, I texted no one more than you. I'm serious. I even thought about switching to unlimited texting because of that. I will miss recapping American Idol after each show. I will miss reminding you that American Idol is not 6-year-old soccer… Everyone is NOT a winner. I will miss you talking about how much you cried watching American Idol each week. To hear us discuss the show you would have thought we were going to become the next set of judges.

I will not, however, miss your yelling. Just so you know, it IS possible to emphasize something without increasing your volume. I will not miss looking at your wardrobe choices and saying, "Yeah, I probably wouldn't wear that to high school."

One of the things I will miss most is your exuberant character. You make people smile, laugh, and cry all at the same time. You have enthusiasm and unlimited energy. You are one of those people who I can't wait to see find themselves. I'm pretty sure that as long as American Idol is still on the air, I will be thinking of you and you will be thinking of me. Shortly followed by a text.

fleen

Chapter Fourteen

2014

Dear Friend,

Swimming is one of those sports that don't rank very high on the glamorous meter. You'll probably find it sandwiched between Canoe Slalom and Modern Pentathlon (I know what a pentathlon is, but what makes it modern?). Seriously, the nature of practicing and competing screams (heavy yawn) <u>boring.</u> Let's make this sport even more glamorous by letting 14-17 year old kids (with no experience) do this at a school (with no pool) at the most ungodly of hours. Oh yea and by the way, you have to study for an hour after school before you party at the pool. Now that sounds like something I'd sign up for in a heartbeat! Yeah right, what happens after that? Do we get to clean the bathroom?

For some strange reason, kids at Cathedral City love doing just that. 61 of them to be exact. If I knew why they kept coming back for more I'd bottle it and give it to every school. All I know is that this is what a few had to say:

- *I love the rush I get when I get a best time or out touch someone at the finish.*
- *I love swim because of the people, our team is definitely one of a kind.*
- *Swim gave me a whole new group of friends and it gave me an opportunity to try my hardest at what I liked to do.*
- *I like swimming because of the drive to improve, the thrill of competition, and the lifetime of memories… swim is not a sport it's a blessing.*
- *I like to push the limits.*
- *I love swim because of the friends I've met, the lessons I've learned, and the many amazing experiences that surround it all.*
- *The memories I've made are priceless.*

Wearing birthday pies on your face, singing in front of people because you forgot something, swimming a 50 in ocean swell waves created by teammates, starting practice by being pushed in the pool (with your school clothes still on), spending a week away from home– training hard but laughing even harder, there are no better testimonials for swimming at Cathedral City.

The reasons kids swim at Cathedral City are pretty much the same reasons I coach. There is no better joy, no better fulfillment, and no better satisfaction than the smiles I see on their faces when they've just done something they didn't think they could do. Take freshman Marilu H. She started out in water polo and after two days told me it was too hard and that she wanted to quit. I told her the same thing I've told many kids over the years because I know it is true, "it gets better." She eventually played a few games with Varsity and by the end of her swim season she would finish with the Varsity team and compete at DVL Finals in 3 events.

If I told you what happened with Marilu was not the norm, I'd be lying. It happens every year. Talent, like character, is always there; it just needs to be revealed.

In some ways, it was a typical year. The Varsity girls would compete well and win most of their meets, doing so with rarely the same lineup. The JV Girls would lose just once and for the 3ʳᵈ year in a row, there would be enough girls to fill a 2ⁿᵈ full JV Girls team. The boys, while very thin with numbers, would compete well and learn throughout the season. What was also typical were the new stars that would be discovered at every turn, like Marilu, Jaiden D, Francisco N, Haidee E, Vanessa A, Jose J Analisia R, Simi C, and Camille M to name a few.

I couldn't imagine a better way to spend an afternoon than to inspire kids who desire to be daily inspired. Thank you for making that possible for both of us.

Swimmingly

❖ The Alligator ❖
Aaron B

I know what you're thinking. What could he possibly say about me that would connect me to an alligator? Those dots cannot be as close as he thinks they are! To those people, I would ask to just listen to this logic. As we all know, alligators possess an amazing skill set. They are long and somewhat sleek, but love food and are not that discriminating. They have a keen sense of their surroundings. They are not good at long distances yet are exceptionally powerful. Finally, you have to admit, they are an 'interesting' looking animal.

Clearly you have no problem with food. I found it hard to believe you once did have a problem in middle school. I honestly thought the "chub" photo was photoshopped. I've heard you talk about food so passionately, that if someone was within earshot and didn't know what you were talking about, they'd swear you were talking about your girlfriend.

You have an incredible intellect and wit. It's not often I field thoughtful questions from student/athletes. You communicate on a level that is both highly intellectual yet non-threatening to kids and adults alike. Combine the two and you get a response like "if I was hungry and had $1, I'd go to COSTCO, eat the samples and donate the money to end world hunger."

You are deceptively strong and quick, yet when asked to swim a 200, you look at me as if the day is not long enough for you to finish. Many ask if it's possible to swim a 25 free. You ask if you can swim a 10.

We all have to admit you have quite a unique style. You must be the only person I know with a hole in his chest who, even though he doesn't need to, still wants to rock a comb-over.

I can only imagine the talent that you would have displayed, the leadership you would have embraced, and the fashion trends you would have created had you swam all four years. I guess those will have to come in the next four years.

fleen

❖ **The Backbone** ❖
Joana R

There is a sameness to coaching swimming. You have water surrounded by four walls, you have a black line, and you have a black T at the end of that line telling you to either turn or to finish. That line is constant, it is dependable, and it is mesmerizing. It is the backbone of swimming. In many ways, you have grown to be the backbone of swim.

To say you were a little quiet when you started is like saying water is a little wet. Like water, you were reliable, efficient, and slowly changing course, but always moving in the right direction. You were noticed and appreciated. That would be the trademark of your character throughout your four years in swim.

Over the next few years, you began to show more and more of yourself and seemingly enjoy swimming more and more as well. You got better and better. This again was noticed and appreciated. Your effort was never far from maximum, your commitment never far from full, and a smile never far from your face. You are like the cute child that no one can be upset with even when they do something wrong.

You always seemed to understand the expectations of the program and rose to meet them on a daily basis. High school kids have their own way of looking at things. It can be endearing and at times frustrating. You have had more than your fair share of endearing moments and very few of the frustrating ones. In short, you have been a pleasure to coach and a pleasure to get to know.

I am so glad you were able to go on the spring break trip this year. When I asked you what you enjoyed about the week you said "getting to know the other swimmers and the coaches better." While I have heard the first half of your comment many times before, I have <u>never</u> heard the second half. I too am grateful for the chance to not only get to know you better that week but for the chance to grow with you these past four years.

fleen

❖ **The Mirror** ❖
Katie B

I t was hard to admit that this day would come. The day I wrote you a senior letter. After all, I've known you for almost half of your life. When I think of you, memories fall like rain. The reflections of who you are, like a mirror, have been a joy to watch. The energetic card runner at swim meets when you were 10. The vibrant cheerleader who others thought was actually on the team when you were 13. The incredibly talented swimmer who would final at DVL every year. The uninhibited beauty others appreciated as genuineness. The girl many envied.

With others, it is difficult to remember specific moments. With you it is easy. I can vividly remember your acting ability on spring break trips, and the expressions on your face. I can remember your unique whine when made to do something you didn't want to do and the deals you tried to broker to get out of it, all under the guise of "it's good for everybody." I can remember the songs you sang (every year) to get your equipment back.

One thing though has me confused. If we were to both look at you in a mirror, the person I would see was not always the person you would see. I can't explain why? I have always thought the world of you. The thought of you graduating made me sad when you were a freshman! You have so many gifts and strengths in so many avenues. I wish you could see the girl I see in the mirror.

As you go on from here, your journey will be uncertain, awkward, and at times mystifying. It is at these moments that I hope you look in the mirror and see the girl we all see. The fun-loving, intuitive, creative, personal, spontaneous, smart, and caring girl, with the world at her feet.

fleen

❖ **The Optimist** ❖
Kayla C

How do you start a letter when emotions are already at the surface? How do you articulate the meaningful impact of a person when they are leaving? How do you show admiration when words cannot suffice? How do you tell an athlete that you have learned more from them than they have learned from you? The only way I know how to… just start.

Your start was different for me. You were the most wide-eyed, OH WOW!, (see open mouth) girl I'd ever seen. Things did not come easy at the beginning, but that didn't seem to bother you. You just kept smiling and plugging along (see Little Engine That Could). To say you are a little optimistic is like saying Batman saved a couple of people. I mean, can someone honestly see something good about adding 120 seconds in a 50 free? You can say, 'at least you finished, you didn't drown, your cap didn't come off, everyone still cheered for you, your suit stayed on, love your fingernails.' Most importantly you meant every word.

I quickly learned that you are that genuine. Kayla C, first and last name required. When someone would complain I'd just send them to Kayla Cooper. When that someone was me, I'd be secretly ashamed and would quickly refocus. When someone needed a pep talk, I'd send them to Kayla C. When that someone was me, (I don't think you ever realized this) I'd seek you out and always feel better after.

Stories will be told about Kayla C in the future. All will be about your remarkable outlook on life. Those who listen may find them hard to fathom. To those people, I will look them straight in the eye and say 'they could not be more true.' I cannot say enough good things about you. You are the light in the dark, the joy in a sea of anguish, the peace in a world of pain. Thank you for being such a positive influence on everyone you have touched, including me.

fleen

❖ **The Line** ❖
Sophia L

I have to admit, you snuck in under the radar. Because we have so many kids and so little space to practice them all I usually don't allow first year seniors to swim. I would rather invest in someone who will be around for a few years. I'm convinced you had a plan all along. It was probably something like this. Sign up in the fall when he wouldn't know who I was, hope his T.A. enters the student info including grade, buy a parka just to ensure my place, and last but not least, act like a freshman. Congratulations! Mission accomplished.

You, like many before you, had no idea what you were getting into. Swimming is difficult and it was clear to see that you and water had some personal issues with each other. Not quite like oil and vinegar, but close. Yet there you were giving it your all. Mind willing and the body just trying to play catch up. Morning practice. You mean I actually have to go sometimes? I didn't see that one coming.

So there you were mid-season continuing to work and continuing to make improvements. You learned to not only swim, but also to cheer, sing, encourage, and laugh. I hope you also learned that even though you snuck in under the radar, you were just as important as everyone else.

For me though, I felt you needed to learn something else. How to respond to compliments. You are smart, attractive, and have a good personality... really! What better way to learn than to have me throw pick-up lines at you, constantly. It's going to happen in the future, so better learn now how to react when they start coming your way. At first, the lines would catch you off guard and you would just smile. Eventually you learned how to respond and hold your own. I wish I could be there in the future, to see you responding to someone saying, "Do you believe in love at first sight or should I walk by again?" They won't know what hit them.

fleen

❖ **The Call** ❖
Tristan P

What I love about people are the differences they each possess. If uniqueness of thought, action, and word were not visible, we would all be the worse for it. It would be like a band performing on stage to no one. They could do it, but we all know it just wouldn't be the same. It is this quality that not only separates but also defines you.

The first difference I noticed was your intelligence. You were book smart, people smart, and athletic smart. I knew that no matter what fell apart at your feet, you could put it back together. On the flip side, your reaction after being shown how something actually worked was usually followed by a very noticeable "duh."

Next is your genetically unrivaled hair. I mean that hair is so long, thick, and weighty you have to pay an extra baggage fee on airplanes. You don't need a pencil pouch; you can keep pens, pencils, and erasers all in your hair. I'm convinced there is a small nest with even smaller creatures living in there that couldn't be happier. When they perform an autopsy on you they'll have to perform a separate one just for your hair.

Your emotions also set you apart. You have some that are clearly near the surface and others that rarely see the light of day. Both reveal your uncommon heart. You are the only person I've known to laugh so boisterously it makes people wonder if that sound came from a human. I've named it The Call of Tristan, with Moose being your moniker. The name was solidified at Claim

Jumper your sophomore year. We walked in and there it was in all its glory… a huge moose head above the fireplace. As loud as your laugh was, if we kept you bellowing long enough, your laugh would turn into a sobbing so emotional you'd have thought every dog on the planet had just passed away.

The final extraordinary thing about you is that you are comfortable in your own skin. You know who you are, what you are about, and you make no apologies. You are not a follower, you are not uncomfortable in difficult situations, and you own your shortfalls.

I am so very proud of you and even more proud to have been a part of your life these past four years. To you I can only say, the best is yet to come.

fleen

❖ The Journey ❖
Vanessa T

One of my favorite quotes is, "Life is a journey, not a destination." To me, it embodies process and experience. Many people spend their whole lives trying to reach a point, a goal, a culmination. The sad thing is, when they reach it they are often left unsatisfied. The reason may be that they have not enjoyed, and many times don't remember, all it took to get there. In a society driven by 'the latest greatest' you, Vanessa, are a breath of fresh air. You, Vanessa, have reached milestones that others might deem uneventful, but we both know are beyond measure.

There are many reasons why I have enjoyed this journey with you these past four years. The fact that you still look like a freshman always takes me back to the beginning. You have continuously demonstrated loyalty. While you may have joined with other people that first year, many of them are gone, but you are still here. You have remained loyal to the program. One of the people you joined with is still here. To her, you have also, remained loyal.

Another part of your journey has been sincerity. Your character has never wavered. You are who you are. Whether it's going from moments of quiet reflection to endless streams of nonstop talking, each is you. You know the value of a positive word and the value of sacrifice. Because of this you have experienced more and will remember more than most others, about your time in swim. I can say the same.

I will remember the way you excitedly tell stories and the awkward way you end them. And I will remember my slightly tilted expression. I will remember the tears you shed as you left your family for the first time on a spring break trip. And I will remember me trying to encourage more of them. I will remember your eyebrows and morning octopus hair. And I will hope that never happens to me.

Thank you for taking me along with you on your journey these past four years.

fleen

❖ **The Real You** ❖
Yesenia G

High school can be a difficult and trying time. It can also be the spark that opens up and helps to create the real you. I think in your case both statements are accurate. Throughout the last four years, you have made choices that have, not only defined, but have revealed the real you.

While you didn't begin high school at Cathedral

City, you courageously made the move after just one semester at another school. As a freshman it is hard to jump into something midstream, yet that is exactly what you did. Your desire to try something new and quickly fit in was my first indication that you were a genuine person. Over the course of the next few years, you would continue to make decisions that would reveal the sincerity of your character, the depth of your commitment, and the genuineness of your spirit.

But it has been the past few years that I have witnessed the most growth. You have gone from that uncertain leader to a passionate example of Cathedral City Swim. Your work ethic, both in and out of the pool, has been an inspiring example to others and me. Your honest reactions to adversity and triumph only solidified your authenticity as a person. When you were confused, you questioned. When you were uncertain, you gave it your all. When you were challenged, you did not back down.

I will miss your silly jokes, your big laugh, your surface emotions, and your pure soul. Most of all I will miss the real you.

fleen

Chapter Fifteen

2015

Dear Friend

Where do you draw the line, your line? Where is the point where inconvenience trumps progress? Where is the point where improvement is smothered in logistics? It is my belief we all have these moments each day. They are, what some like to call, the consistent battles within. We weigh the risk and reward and quickly decide and do. While some battles are resolved and won immediately, others take time and the outcome is uncertain. So we ask ourselves, when do we throw in the towel and say it can't be done, that reward is not worth the effort?

Two battles have waged for the last 24 years. The first has been fought some 8760 times by more than 850 people and is still being fought today. These people have chosen to fight this battle and they have done so with tired eyes, weary bodies, and smiles on their faces. Who are these people? They are Cathedral City swimmers. Imagine this is what awaits you as a prospective swimmer your freshman year.

Daily Schedule
4:45am - wake up
5:15-6:45am - practice
7:15 - breakfast in room 210
8:00am-2:54pm - School
3:00-4:00pm - study hall
4:10pm - catch bus to practice
4:30-4:45pm - dry land
5:00-7:00pm- practice
7:30pm - return to school by bus
7:45pm - arrive home for dinner

Following tryouts, no one will be cut. In addition, whether you are a first year swimmer with no experience or a 4th year swimmer preparing to swim in college, the coaches' expectations for you will be the same. Be on time, fulfill your academic and practice requirements, represent your school, your team, your family, and yourself with pride.

I don't know of many adults who would choose such a schedule. Yet for some reason swimmers at

Cathedral City have chosen this for the last 24 years. They've never known any other way. Talent, or lack thereof, has had very little to do with their success. The commitment they make on a daily basis, the battles within they choose to win each day, has had everything to do with their success.

The other battle was won Oct 27 2014 when the board of education approved the construction of a district aquatic center on the campus of Cathedral City High School. I have tried for years to encourage the district that this was an important and worthy project. For them to finally agree, made it a momentous day for me, my athletes' past and present, their families, the school, the city, and the district. I am thrilled that future swimmers will have a place to call 'home.' I imagine the pool will be ready sometime in the Fall of 2016.

As usual some 55 swimmers, 20 of which were new to the program, had another memorable season. New swimmers found themselves on Varsity at some point (see Alex V, Noelia M, Angela I, and Isabel C), three would qualify for CIF (see Chris C, Marco P and Arysa L). In addition, 16 swimmers had a fantastic week of sight-seeing, training, and fun in Flagstaff, Arizona. Training indoors at elevation (7000 ft) on the campus of Northern

Arizona University provided a perfect backdrop to an amazing week. The team was also shown the campus of Arizona State University by former athlete Kim S. They visited Sedona and the Grand Canyon. They spent an afternoon at a high rope park climbing across roped obstacles and sliding along zip lines in the trees. They also visited Slide Rock State Park jumping off ledges and sliding down rocks. The swimmers loved the all-you-can-eat concept of dining in college. The fun-filled team activities were won by team Cisco and the Fish.

Our graduating seniors will be moving on in many positive directions. Marco P will be swimming and playing polo at Mt San Antonio College, Chris C is enlisting in the Coast Guard, Vanessa M will attend the University of Hawaii, Gissell V - Cal State Long Beach, Jessie V - UC Irvine, and Alex F Cal State Fullerton. Alex was also chosen as the Palm Springs Boys and Girls Club Youth of the Year. For that he will receive a $30,000 scholarship.

I want to thank you again for supporting the swim program at Cathedral City and offering my student-athletes the chance to win so many important daily battles.

Swimmingly

❖ **The Brain** ❖
Alex F

They say we only use 10% of our brain. While I don't know if that is true, I do know that is a little disappointing. I've always wondered how such an incredibly made organ can be so widely valued yet so underused. The team once had a valedictorian who couldn't pump her own gas. Really?...how does that happen? I've come to realize that much more goes on inside the brain, inside your brain, than most of us know.

While you have always been a good student, what I have come to appreciate about you is that you simply try and you care. You put yourself out there and you do the best you can. Whether academically, musically, or athletically you simply try and you care and it shows. I'm sure the B's you received in 6th grade math still irritate you, I'm sure the notes you miss in band still irritate you, I'm sure the fact that you still swim with your head too high in backstroke irritates you, and I'm sure the vision of others not trying or caring irritates you.

The brain of the average high school student tends to spend too much time in the Limbic system, the emotional center of the brain, and not the Cerebrum, the cognitive part. Throughout high school, you seemed to have taken advantage of the cognitive portion of your brain that focuses on learning & memory, decision making, and perception. I think your peers have recognized this, your teachers have recognized this, the Boys & Girls Club has recognized this, and your swim coach has recognized this. It is what separates you from the crowd. It is what will put you at the front of the line.

While that valedictorian probably still can't pump her own gas, while I continue to misspell 'the' every time I type it, and while you will probably still swim backstroke with your head too high, it is OK. I'm confident the three of us use at least 11% of our brain.

fleen

❖ **The Voice** ❖
Gissel V

As you became a senior I began to think about the letter I would write you. Being a four-year senior made it even more special. Multiple scenarios ran through my mind. I honestly didn't know where to start. In many ways, you represent what is important about being a Lion swimmer. You are dependable, conscientious, trustworthy, and loyal. You are also smart, committed to your music, you stalk celebrities, and (sorry mom & dad) you drive too fast. You are a rare breed.

We both know you are quiet. When you were asked to write something most people don't know about you, you wrote "I talk". I jokingly thought I would write more words to you than you said to me in four years. When I talk to others I wait for the usual verbal response, with you I wait for the usual nonverbal response. At first, it was difficult for me to see if you understood what I was trying to explain. Your facial expressions were like desert weather, pretty much the same every day. I slowly learned how to distinguish the looks. To most your expressions are indistinguishable. Over time I learned the subtle differences your looks conveyed. A millimeter one direction meant "I got you coach" a millimeter the other direction meant "I'll figure it out myself." I was left satisfied either way. Over time affirmative nods became "ahuh," "ahuh" then soon became "yes." I almost cried the first time I heard "yes." Then I learned you stalk Kim Kardashian. I'll be honest, I was both surprised and impressed. Then I saw you drive and I feared for my life.

One thing I have learned about you is you know who you are. At the end of the day that is the most important thing. I am not worried about where you will go from here, I am confident you will be more than successful.

I do want to remind you though... When you decide to get married, you <u>will</u> have to <u>say</u> your vows, you won't be able to nod them.

fleen

❖ **The Story** ❖
Jessie V

Movies are a staple of most people's lives. It's a place to get away from our own reality, if only for a few hours. Movies tell a story. There are usually a host of characters involved, each with their own story. We are intrigued, fascinated, curious, and confused by certain characters which is exactly why we keep watching. We want to know how it ends. Throughout your four years in swim I have seen you exhibit all of the aforementioned character qualities. Like a good movie, I have enjoyed it immensely and eagerly wait for the end. I also know the unfortunate truth. Your movie is far from over and your characters will certainly change from here.

Here are some of my favorite characters.

The Student. With the exception of a small bump in the road this year, your academics were never a cause for worry or concern. I hope you know how much I appreciated your commitment to school. Looking at your grades always made me smile.

The Comedian. Like a martini, you like your comedy dry. Your quick wit could only be matched by your flawless delivery. Whether you started it or I did, conversations had a way of bordering the ridiculous with an unrecognizable smell of reality. Bystanders, usually underclassmen, were often left asking "are they serious?"

The Performer. This side you kept hidden for quite some time. When I finally witnessed the phenomenon, I was speechless. I honestly didn't know your voice could sound or your body could move like they did. Very impressive.

The Ambassador. Like many before you, you have represented all I feel is important about swim. You are dedicated, fun-loving, genuine, concerned, and respectful. For this I am grateful.

While I do not know how your story will end, I am confident in saying that most of characteristics that are you, will provide those watching, with a plot twist they didn't see coming and won't soon forget.

fleen

❖ **The Dent** ❖
Marco P

We all love new things. New clothes, new phones, new experiences, and new girlfriends. At some point in our lives, we will experience the joy of our first new car (Attention, you will need to get a driver's license at some point). When we drive it off the lot with a huge smile and take the long way home showing it off to as many people as possible along the way. We'll wash it every day, friends will have to remove their shoes upon entering, food is forbidden, and anyone altering the distribution of music will be asked to leave immediately.

Then one day you find a dent in the door. Worse yet, you put it there. You try to ignore it, but everyone sees it and most remind you of it incessantly. What many lose sight of is the fact that the dent is small in comparison to the size of the car and it really can be fixed at any time. The people you meet in the future would never even know there was ever a dent in the door.

High school for you has been your new car. It looked amazing your first year. Then as fate would have it, you found some dents. Worse yet, you put them there. Not being able to swim one year made you realize how much you valued your car. Getting around on a skateboard just wasn't the same (see broken arm). I am thrilled you got your car back and it looks great.

While your car was taken away, it still ran well and 99% of it was awesome. It was just waiting for you. Having known you for so long it has been a joy to see you grow in so many positive ways. While I saw the dent, I also saw that 99% of you was special. As you move on to college I am confident you have learned how to keep your car running smoothly and dent free.

fleen

❖ **The Marker** ❖
Vanessa M

High school is filled with breakthrough moments, those amazing signature events. Your first 'A' in school, a beautiful sunrise, a break through time in swim, your first kiss (I'll assume they've all happened). Those moments are the markers that define us, the ones we carry with us the rest of our lives. I have no doubt you have many.

One marker... I remember it like it was yesterday. When I first heard it I smiled, then I laughed, then I cried because I was laughing so hard. What, you ask, am I referring to? I am naturally referring to your laugh. The first time I heard it I couldn't believe it was yours. Like a shirt too small, it just didn't seem to fit you. We were in Portland when it happened. Like a call in the wild, I heard it but did not know who it belonged to. It sounded like a sputtering moped that changed pitch. When I learned it came from you, I, like many others, was picking my chin up off the ground. To my astonishment, it kept coming. It didn't stop. Soon thereafter, like Paris Hilton and a camera, I couldn't get enough. It became a drug for me and I needed it, all the time. My quest for the rest of the week was to make you laugh. That marker, your marker, was honestly one of the highlights of the week.

While I will not soon forget your laugh, there are many other makers I will remember. Your willingness to be involved, your concern for others, your integrity, and you are but a few. As a coach, I can only hope I have instilled a sense of belongingness that will encourage athletes to try, to learn, to seek, and to leave a marker. Thank you for leaving your marker with me.

fleen

Chapter Sixteen

2016

Dear Friend

It is not often that you have the chance to reinvent yourself. To put a new face on something that everyone else has seen a thousand times. Yet that is exactly what will happen in the spring of 2017. A new pool will be built on the campus of Cathedral City High School and for the first time in school history home pool advantage will actually mean something.

Three grade levels will be a part of the present and future. They will have swum at the Palm Springs Swim Center and will swim in the new district Aquatic Center. They will have understood the extra level of commitment required to be a Cathedral City swimmer. They will also understand and appreciate the ability to walk to practice after school instead of taking a bus.

Once again those challenges did not prevent 40 swimmers from having another memorable season. While the number of boys dipped a little this year, the girls' numbers remained strong. As usual, many new swimmers discovered their hidden talent. Freshmen Sara A and Sierra S produced amazing results and Josh F would do the same for the boys. Sara A would be a consistent contributor on Varsity all season. By the end of the season Sierra S, with no prior competitive swimming experience, would swim Varsity and Final at DVL in the 100 breaststroke. Josh F would also make it to DVL in the breaststroke. That is very difficult to do considering the presence of club swimmers throughout the other DVL schools.

The sophomore class would have to go down as the most improved group. Again, all had no swimming experience prior to high school yet many would demonstrate tremendous improvement throughout the season. Carolina C, Isabel C, Angela I, Gillian M, and Belen O would come to provide the backbone of the Varsity Squad. Junior Marilu H proved to be the most accomplished. She would narrowly miss CIF qualifying times in the 100 fly and 100 back at DVL finals.

Seniors Kenya F, Rosa H, Marrissa J, Janet M, Ana R, and Karina V would be the glue holding the team together. The experience and leadership they provided was essential to the growth and development of the team.

On the boys' side, juniors Sebastian G and DeVon T led the way in many meets. Competing again teams with more boys, while difficult from a scoring standpoint, didn't dampen their competitive spirit.

Santa Barbara provided the backdrop to another incredible spring break trip. The training, the team activities, the college visits, and the laughter won't soon be forgotten.

I want to thank you again for supporting the student-athletes at Cathedral City. I also want to be the first to invite you to come watch us swim in 2017 in our new pool. With your support. I know home pool advantage will finally mean something.

Swimmingly

❖ **The Old Soul** ❖
Analisia R

I lived in the 80's. I have to admit, it was a good time for many things. Movies, fashion, and music were all trending in multiple directions. The decade was a little confused, a little off-balance, a little mesmerizing, and definitely unforgettable. If you're looking for a party theme, look no further. Whether you lived it or not, everyone knows the 80's. Ana R, I'm convinced you were born in the wrong generation. Most of what I know about you does not scream 2000's. Your values, concern for others, musical taste, and aura are uniquely misplaced.

I love the story about why people swim. While you may have your version, I'm convinced you swam because I coached your mom. It was in the genes. Your mom was born close enough to the '80s to be a member and so you too are a member. Things happened in the '80s that defied explanation, but to this day we remember some of those things.

When you chose to swim, or as I like to say, when swim chose you, your first few steps were like a newborn doe. A little confused, a little off balance. Yet you persevered and continued to move forward, step by step, stroke by stroke. When you gravitated towards fly your junior year, you were mesmerizing to watch. The stroke looked so natural. While it probably didn't 'feel' so natural, your stroke was a joy to watch.

As you grew, you learned what swimming at Cathedral City is all about, it was about feeling discomfort to discover your comfort. Many things about you are unforgettable: Your "I got this" and your "it's so cold", your "I love singing" and your "just not in front of people", and your morning DJ moments. How you know more songs from that generation than I do, I'll never know, but I loved the way it woke you up and made you smile.

I will miss the old soul that I came to know, but more than that, I will miss your new soul as you move on from here.

fleen

❖ **The Shining** ❖
Janet M

When I look back on my time with you, I will think of the shining. Not the 1980 horror film starring Jack Nicholson, but the always present smile that shines like a beacon from your face. Some say your smile is the window to your soul. If that is indeed the case, then you Janet M, have a beautiful soul.

As a freshman, the smile made its initial public offering on March 5th against Perris. Like most, you were extremely nervous. Your nervousness doubled as you discovered your first ever race would be the 500 Free. While I don't remember the details, I'm sure you smiled before, during, and after to hide the pain. I'm also sure you smiled in your next race, the 50 back, which you would DQ.

While many practices, races, and team activities would follow in the next four years, the common denominator in all would be your smile. I can't tell you how much I appreciate your attitude, your positivity, your resilience, your commitment, and most importantly your smile. I was so happy to share the spring break experience with you. Mostly because I knew you would appreciate the moments as they came each day.

Smiles need no explanation or translation.
They are infectious and free.

They reveal more than you think.
Yours will always be with me.

You will take many memories with you as you leave, in addition to your smile. Thank you for leaving with me the memory of all you have done, for it is that which will always make <u>me</u> smile.

fleen

❖ **The Carnival** ❖
Karina V

As a kid, I loved carnivals. Who doesn't love carnivals? The food, the rides, the shows, and my favorite, the games. l learned quickly not to go to the games first. If I did, I never saw anything else. I'd literally spend the whole day playing games, sometimes one game. And for what, a giant Giraffe! But I couldn't pass up the challenge. I loved the 'knock it over' games, but my favorite was the shooting game. Various objects moving across a backdrop, usually a sweet looking baby chick, and all I had to do was hit it? Count me in! I love the challenge.

I was recently asked if a student had ever made me want to quit teaching or coaching. I laughed and said 'no'. I said no for the same reason I like shooting games, I love the challenge and I don't take it personally.

Enter Karina V. She, of wonderful sense of humor. She, of uncanny wit. She, of intellectual curiosity. She, of adventurous spirit. She, of incredible athletic talent. She, of fiercely competitive nature. She, of fiercely competitive nature. She, of fiercely competitive nature. You get the idea.

To coach you was like the shooting game. It looks so easy. Just shoot the little chick. Then I quickly realized sometimes it was just the opposite. I wouldn't have wanted it any other way. After all, I love the challenge. I understand high school is a time of growing and learning, and not just for the kids. Sometimes we can be our own worst enemy.

The good news for me was you showed your emotions like a clown shows a painted face. In my opinion, you would be a terrible poker player.

As happy as you made me sometimes (heavy sarcasm detected) you were an invaluable asset to the team. The team needed you and I needed you.

In you I honestly see unlimited potential to do and be anything you want. You possess the necessary qualities. Use those qualities to your advantage.

fleen

❖ **The Weaver** ❖
Kenya F

Stone by stone. Brick by brick. Stitch by stitch. Things have to begin from something. A thought, an idea, something has to inspire the next move. Once that first move has been made, every move after must be woven together. This is the hard part. It is not easy to find the right weaver. The ability to integrate, be precise, enjoy, and care. For the past four years, you have been instrumental in maintaining the fabric of Cathedral City Swim. You, Kenya F, are a weaver.

Integrating the demands of academics, sports, ASB, and HEAL was not easy. Yet you seamlessly wove the demands of each while not compromising the integrity of any. You wore each fabric well.

Precision and detail are what separates the good weaver from the great one. We all are involved in something. But it is the one who understands the importance of precision that is the one people flock to for something woven. The difference in the fabric can be easily seen and never mistaken for anything other than quality. Your attention to detail is what has made you a successful weaver.

The best job is one that does not feel like work. You can't fake real. The joy you show while weaving is palpable. Others see it and wish they had your sense of amusement. Your singing, laughing, and storytelling are like a flashlight in a dark room that lights the path for others wanting to follow.

Caring about the fabric is the unseen, yet possibly the most important, quality of a good weaver. The ability to care is like fine art, you know it when you see it. You are a fine weaver.

In a time where accomplishment takes precedence over striving, finding a good weaver must be appreciated because they don't last forever, though the memory of you may be remembered for nearly that long.

fleen

❧ **The 'B' Team** ❧
Marrissa J

I love it. Everyone has to start somewhere. Truth be told, it is one of my favorite places. Tucked somewhere between fear and nervous anxiety lies the 'B' team. <u>The beginning</u>. I still remember my first pro triathlon starting line. I still remember my band's first gig. I still remember my first day of teaching. I have come to know it is the best place to be.

For you, it was the 'JV B team.' Your fellow seniors, Janet and Ana, shared the stage with you that first day. They with their 1:50 100 splits, and you the speedster, with your blazing 1:39. Smiles, laughter, and hyperventilating moments later would be the lasting memory of only one thing. <u>The beginning</u>.

Year two your start would be 'JV A.' There was a JV B team, but for you it was a distant past, a memory preserved. Your Freestyle would be faster, your cheers louder, and your enthusiasm infectious. To the casual observer, nothing was new, but we both know everything was new. It was called <u>the beginning</u>.

Two years would pass in the blink of an eye and while you are now called a veteran, the start still feels as close as a band -aid on a cut. It is exhilarating and exhausting, fast and furious, real and rewarding. It still feels like <u>the beginning</u>.

The nice thing about new beginnings is it gives us a clearer perspective of growth, accomplishment, and fear. I appreciate you accepting every new beginning I gave you, and in turn, giving those same new beginnings to other swimmers as they came into the program. I will always appreciate and miss our beginning conversations each day. The one where you look me in the eye and sincerely ask… "how was your day?"

fleen

❖ **The Apple** ❖
Rosa H

I t is safe to say that in the last 30 years there have been more technological advances than in the last 300. The time between "I gotta have that" and "you still have one of those?" has shrunk significantly. At the forefront of change in the eyes of many has been Apple. Their innovative devices, creative applications, and sleek designs are the envy of many. To paraphrase Steve Jobs "it is my job to convince people to buy something they didn't know they needed."

I met you as a sophomore when, at the urging of friends, you decided to swim and play polo. I didn't know much about you, but I liked your energy. You were very committed and seemed to enjoy the whole aquatic thing. In your junior year you began to realize, not only your potential, but your limitations. Nothing appeared to stop you at all. To say that I now knew a lot about you would be a misrepresentation. As your senior year began I saw this passion for all things aquatic. You wanted to be a part of everything. And I mean everything! You appeared to find something you were good at, and because it would be your last go around, you didn't want to miss anything.

I have to be honest with you. I think you Steve Jobbed me. You became that thing I didn't know I needed but now can't live without. That innovative device, that creative application, that sleek design. I always thought you were a great person, but in the last two months I realized how truly kind, giving, dedicated, funny, and charming you are. You made me realize how important you are to the program. And now that I realize how important you are, you are leaving.

Not to worry, while trends may come and go, in my 'Rosa Museum' I still have the following. 1. Your multiple editorial performances. 2. Your witty and hilarious comments. 3. Your many, many, many petable moments. 4. The memory of a truly amazing person.

fleen

Chapter Seventeen

2017

Dear Friends,

Have you ever wanted something—wanted something so bad—only to be told no, again and again and again. No matter how you presented it, it didn't seem to matter; the answer was always the same: no. You did all the leg work, disseminated the appropriate information, demonstrated the need, and outlined in detail the reasons why, yet the answer was still no. Then, one day, you had a sliver of hope. Someone believed in you, believed in your mission, and shared your passion. Suddenly, the answer was yes. If this has ever happened to you, then I think you know how I feel.

The pool on the campus of Cathedral City High School is more than just a pool. It is a dream come true, not just for myself, but for future generations of high school student-athletes and kids of all ages. That pool that was in the back of my head for so many years now stands before me each and every day. It is beautiful, but not ostentatious; functional, but not frilly; dynamic, but not lacking. It is everything I imagined and more.

January 9th, 2017 will be a day forever etched into my mind. My athletes were able to experience for themselves what they had seen being built before their very eyes for the previous 7 months. Their smiles could not have been bigger. We were able to finish the girls' water polo season in the new pool.

Swim would start February 1st. What I imagined would happen did indeed happen. 80 swimmers, the largest team in school history and by far the largest team in the valley, would begin the 27th and first edition of Cathedral City Swim. It was an exciting time in that I had the privilege to see so many new faces begin a memorable journey, many of whom would become far better than they imagined. The girls would field two levels of JV swimmers for each meet. Even so, it was sometimes difficult to find enough swims for everyone. Two first-year swimmers would even make it to the DVL league meet: sophomore Maria M in the 100 Fly and Freshman Kenna I in the 100 Breast. Both were and are rising stars.

The girls' team would make CIF cuts in multiple events led by senior Marilu H who had cuts in the 100 back and 200 Free, junior Angela I in the 100 Fly, and sophomore Sierra S in the 100 Breast. Those three, plus senior Julie C, would also make a cut in the 200 Medley Relay. It was so much fun to watch those and others like sophomores Sara A, AnAvy B, juniors Carolina C, Isabel C, Gillian M, and Belen O have such a positive impact.

For the boy', junior Blake G would just miss a cut in the 50 Free. Seniors Sebastian G and DeVon T were solid all season long. Freshmen Bernardo N and Jesus V improved with every meet. While small, the boys' team showed the talent was there. The problem they had was having the appropriate depth throughout the lineup.

The Desert Valley League Prelims/Finals were held at our pool as well. With the stands full and over 200 swimmers crowding the deck, it was a sight to see. The sounds of cheering fans and screaming athletes could be heard everywhere. The athletes enjoyed seeing their names posted on the new digital display board. Each swimmer finished their race hoping to see a 1 next to their name as the winner. Words can't describe the energy and enthusiasm in the air those two days.

Thank you to everyone over the last 27 years; athletes, parents, and donors alike, who helped create the unique culture that is Cathedral City Swim. I hope you have the chance one day to stop and see for yourself.

Swimmingly

❖ **The Reason** ❖
Andrea C

I love the people who've got it figured out. The ones just passing through high school on their way to bigger and better. The ones listening with one ear and preparing their response to a comment with the other. The ones whose logic is clear to them, and usually only them. There is a perfectly good reason for...

I'm sure there was reason why you wore your hair the way you did underneath your cap. Maybe it was because you thought you had a crazy amount of hair. Maybe you just liked it that way. When I tried to tell you there was another way, I quickly learned you had a reason why. So I stopped trying and called you antenna.

I'm sure there was a reason why you spent so much time in front of the closet mirror preparing your alter ego in my room after morning practice. I tried to tell you natural was better. That you were beautiful just the way you are. My comments were usually met with "you don't understand." There was a reason. When I saw you choose make-up over food I didn't even try to understand. There was a reason. One of my favorite mornings was the lesson I received about cheek makeup. While I quickly forgot the technical term, it apparently gives you high cheekbones, and apparently that is important. There was a reason.

I often wondered why you chose to do swim and polo for a coach with high expectations. Maybe I learned from you that while you always had a reason, sometimes the reason didn't matter. Thank you for reminding me I don't always need to know why. The fact that you were dedicated, honorable, and kind became reason enough.

fleen

❖ **The Dive** ❖
Dania M

I am one of the luckiest people I know. I get to go to a job that guarantees I will not experience the same thing each day. Words like office and cubicle might as well be synonyms for jail. Who gets to interact with adults in training and get paid for it? What did I do to deserve this? What did I do to deserve you?

You, Dania M, are just entertaining to watch. I really am irrelevant. I might be there, but you don't need me. Your thoughts are already programmed and your responses pre-approved, by you of course. I loved listening to you interact with your friends and with me. I felt like I was on the outside looking in. You never lacked an opinion which is why your future is so bright. As convinced as you are of your own path of perception, you also have this willingness to slowly let people inside. You listen, you ponder, and in those rare instances, you have been known to utter "I get you." You are both stubborn and open-minded, unabashed and meek, loud and unassuming, fearless and fearful.

Your talents range from confidence to fashion, from academic prowess to a sparkling spirit, and from fun seeker to diver. Yes, diving. Perhaps that is why I deserve you. Watching you be committed, over the years, to all you do was a joy. I am reminded of that joy every time I watch you dive.

fleen

❖ **The Time Machine** ❖
DeVon T

We are all given gifts and talents. It is what we do with them that defines us. High School is a unique period of time. But unlike a time machine, when we look back, we don't always see the same things. Some see four years of learning, others see growth. While still others see discovery, achievement, and celebration. They are a constant reminder of the flashbacks that are high school. What will you see?

For me, that question remains to be determined. You possess many amazing attributes. Drive, intelligence, wit, and talent are but a few. Seeing you carry a difficult academic load while pursuing your extracurricular passions was an inspiration. Perhaps that is why one day you went to practice only to spend it sleeping in your car when you arrived. Those special days remind us just how special we are.

The glimpses of greatness, the flashes of understanding, and the glances of humility. I think that is some of what I will remember. We should all be so fortunate. I am excited for you, knowing the qualities you have been blessed with. I look forward to hearing stories from your mom about what you have accomplished and how. Your time machine will be an interesting one to look back upon.

fleen

❖ The Mountains ❖
Jennifer P

Without really realizing it, I've always been surrounded by mountains. Whether in Oregon, Santa Barbara, Switzerland, or here in the desert, mountains have been a steady constant. I take it for granted that they will always surround me. I remember a trip to Iowa one year. One of my first impressions was how barren it appeared. There were no mountains and there was barely any elevation change. I couldn't understand how people could live there. I mean, what did they look at when they went outside?

Mountains are unique, evoke wonder, provide an amazing backdrop for adventure, and no two are the same. In some ways, you are a bit like mountains. Over the past three years, you have been a steady constant in swim. I have enjoyed watching you struggle, improve, and experience the fruits of your labor. Your efforts did not go unnoticed and ultimately became inspiration for others. Your smile, like your singing and acting ability, is unique. All are quite the show, but in all honesty, I prefer the smile.

While mountains may not look to change, up close we can see new and special nuances that leave us speechless. Throughout the years I have discovered your commitment, determination, quality of character, and desire to be your best. You have been a willing supporter and, when the situation called for one, also a victim. Whether in school or in swim, you cared enough to try.

For those qualities, I am grateful to have witnessed the unique wonder you possess. I am also anxious to see your uniqueness, wonder, and adventure in full display over the next four years.

fleen

❖ **The Virus** ❖
Julie C

nfectious: likely to spread or influence others in a rapid manner. Synonyms: irresistible, compelling, persuasive, contagious. When talking about a disease, these words are not something you want to hear. In a twist of ironic fate, when you look at the synonyms, most of us would want those words to describe us. When you look at it like that, who wouldn't want to be infectious? There are people and there are infectious people. I think we both know where you fall on the spectrum.

You first infected everyone as a freshman. Carrying the same disease as your sister, it touched us all. The symptoms were laughter, unabridged enthusiasm, connectedness, and goofball-ness. Yes, goofball-ness is real. Your singing, dancing, flower headband wearing, willingness to try anything spirit could not be contained. Others secretly wished they could also have the virus.

Then as quickly as it came, it disappeared. As a coach, I understood why it was so important to have the virus. It transforms normal people into fearless ones, it spreads easily through contact, and it can not be stopped. I could not replicate it nor could find it. The few people that have it are the kinds of people others aspire to. Others secretly dream of being as sick as you.

Then out of nowhere, the virus returned. At a distance I could see it, once again, spread uncontrollably. But somehow the virus had morphed. Yes, it still possessed the same symptoms as before, but now it showed traits of maturity, leadership, and inclusiveness.

I wish I could bottle the virus and give it to every future swimmer. I would administer it with the biggest needle possible and tell them, "at first it might feel a little uncomfortable, but it will ultimately change your life if you let it." I am confident you will continue to infect people for the rest of your life.

fleen

❖ The Ashes ❖
Marilu H

Humble beginnings are the staple of every swimmer at Cathedral City. "From the Ashes", as they say. People join for hundreds of reasons with most being based in fantasy. The reality is that it's not as easy as it looks. Your beginning was more than humble and the reason you started was most likely pure fantasy, which is probably the reason you wanted to quit. I distinctly remember the day you stepped into my office (the back room) and told me you wanted to stop. I also remember my long-winded answer, "you can't." From that moment I have felt nothing but extreme pride for the student you have become, for the athlete you have become, and for the person you have become.

Most of us measure life by the moments we create. Those moments make us laugh, cry, struggle, and make us proud of ourselves. I can't imagine where you or I would be if you had followed through on your first thought. Over the last four years, you have made me laugh, cry, struggle, and made me proud of myself. I hope I have done the same for you. You are the reason

I will never cut anyone and why I try to not let anyone quit.

I won't remember your struggle, I will remember your growth. I won't remember your swim times, I will remember your laughter. I won't remember your frustration, I will remember your passion. Most importantly I will always remember you. I have thoroughly enjoyed pushing you to greater heights and I hope I have the chance to continue to do so after you walk off this stage tonight. My hope is that you realize the talents you possess and the future that waits for you. For out of your ashes, more beauty is waiting to be discovered.

fleen

❖ **The Start** ❖
Nancy E

I love the start. The start of anything and everything. You can never get it back. The good thing is it provides stories to tell your children one day of those auspicious beginnings. I remember teaching one day that first year with my zipper wide open. I remember dropping a stick at the most inopportune time in a song. I remember running off course in a triathlon.

When you started, I remember you swimming for quite some time with your goggles in your mouth, more than once. I remember those dives the judges gave 10's for. But was the score for its perfection or for its entertainment?

I also remember your heart. 'What a good heart,' I thought to myself on more than one occasion. Watching you stick with it while encouraging others at the same time was inspiring. Smiles and positiveness are contagious and you freely gave both at the start of that second year. Your swimming improved and with it your confidence. As a coach that is all I can ask for.

Those starts continued as I learned more about your family, your musical tastes, and the fact that you are not as quiet and shy as I once thought. You are a smart, educated, goal-driven, inspiring soul. After a year off, I am glad you decided to swim again. I enjoyed watching you swim and inspire yet again.

I am so excited for the next chapter of your life. I can't wait to hear the stories of the many firsts that wait for you. When you come back to visit, just throw your O and start talking.

fleen

✧ **The Puzzle** ✧
Sebastian G

Doesn't everyone like a good puzzle? It is one of the most unique pastimes. You don't need special training and anyone can do it. Large or small, simple or complex, puzzles stimulate the mind, engage the participant, and give that sense of satisfaction when completed. Wait, that sounds a lot like being a swimmer at Cathedral City. You, Sebastian G, are a puzzle.

Your freshman year, your puzzle was small. There weren't many pieces and they were pretty big so it was easy to solve. You were eager, enthusiastic, smiled a lot, and clearly had trouble diving with goggles. Perhaps you didn't eat lunch and needed something to put in your mouth. But during the race?

In your sophomore year, the puzzle quickly became larger. Many practice pieces earned you Swimmer of the Week. Even more pieces exposed your musical and theatrical talents. While it took a bit more time to complete, it was worthwhile continuing to try and solve.

The previously mentioned traits only made the puzzle more complicated in your junior year. Throw in your DATA abilities and it was clear you were not the average high school student-athlete. Your ability to engage, enjoy and encourage others made your puzzle even more unique. It seems that just when you thought the puzzle was complete, there were more pieces to place.

I'm curious just how complicated your puzzle will be in the future? I'm relatively certain it will not fit on your average table. As you move on from here I want to thank you for the puzzle you have left. I will look at it in the future and feel like it's still a work in progress.

fleen

Chapter Eighteen

2018

Dear Friend,

28 years is a long time to do anything let alone coach a swim team. We often hear the expression "where did the years go?" and often the quick and simple answer is "I don't know." When we are younger the days, months, and years seem to last forever. As we become older, days feel like months, months feel like years, and years feel like decades. Where did the time go? Although it was just over a year ago when we all stood on deck for the grand opening, the pool feels like it has been there forever. What hasn't changed is the look on people's faces when they see the pool for the first time. After they pick up their jaw, they tell me they've not seen a pool this nice in a long time.

I am very proud of the pool and my athletes are grateful each day they get to use it.

The 2018 Version of Cathedral City Swim picked up right where the 2017 team finished. That energy led to new athletes trying swim for the first time. As is usually the case, many discovered they were pretty good. Names like Orion M, Mauricio V, Fernando G, and Jeremy M proved invaluable for the boys' team. They each brought a unique talent to strengthen the small boys' team. Returning senior Sam R, in addition to sophomores Bernardo N and Jesus V, provided the necessary leadership to make the team much more competitive.

Once again, total numbers would not be a problem for the girls. Over 50 girls contributed to an outstanding season. The JV girls team would lose just once. Many found out that swim was "really fun" and that they were "really good at it." Some of the newcomers would have an opportunity to swim Varsity at some point during the season. While they may have been nervous, their swims demonstrated the opposite. They all performed exceptionally well. Girls like Tais C, Jasmine L, and Kassandra R made drastic improvements throughout the season. Each would make DVL Finals, Tais, and Kassandra in Freestyle and Jasmine in Breaststroke.

It was so fun watching the Varsity Girls team compete each week. There were many meets a year ago that I had a pretty good idea of the outcome. The opposite was true this year. I knew we had some pretty good swimmers, but I also knew that many of the meets would come down to who had the best team. I'm proud to say that we were able to win more than a few meets because of our overall depth. I love it when a meet comes down to the last event. When those situations presented themselves, the girls didn't blink. They embraced the challenge and rose to the occasion. Leadership and experience were not lacking. Sara A, Carolina C, Stephanie H, Angela & Kenna I, Jackie "Bling Bling" L, Maria M, Gillian M, and Sierra S formed the nucleus of the team. Individually Angela I, Sierra S, and the 200 Medley Relay would all make cuts for CIF. Sierra is definitely a star on the rise.

So yes, 28 years is a long time to be doing virtually the same thing. I honestly find myself asking that very question, "where did the time go?" While the "I don't know" answer also floats from my mouth, the thought of those 28 years and the many moments I have had the pleasure of sharing with so many student-athletes only make me smile. Thank all of you for helping to continue the tradition that has become Cathedral City Swim.

Swimmingly

❖ **The Affect** ❖
Citlali C

It is sometimes difficult to put into words how some people have affected you. You'd think it would be easier. After all, you've spent countless hours, days, weeks, and years with this person. Along the way, you've come to learn special things about them.

I have learned you care about your future. You have been diligent in your classes and as a result, you have laid a tremendous foundation for college.

I have learned you are committed. Swimming is not easy and I am not easy. Yet you have understood both and done your best to improve your ability and to please me.

I have learned you have amazing qualities. Your smile can light up a room. It comes easy and often. Your hair, I won't say where, is a wonder in and of itself. It also seems to come easy and often.

I have learned you have goals for yourself. Those goals have been academic, athletic, and personal. More importantly, it appears many have been achieved.

I do not worry about your future. I'm actually excited for you. Not because I know who you are, but because you know who you are.

Thank you for having an effect on me.

fleen

❖ The Rollers ❖
Carolina C

Everyone knows I'm a fan of cycling. I have done it for so long, I can't imagine a life without a bike. I love the exercise, the ability to talk with friends while riding, to experience beautiful nature as it slowly passes my view, and the feeling of accomplishment. Flat roads are mindless and easy, mountains are tough and challenging, but rollers are what create true passion. Rollers are those long roads with small climbs and short descents, one after another. Kind of like a roller coaster without the turns. When I think of you I imagine 4 years of rollers.

When you started you were a bit shy. You weren't quite like the other kids. Somehow you held your own and made it through the early stages of learning strokes, how to be a teammate, and how to communicate without coming across as aloof. The roller was a small, but important one. It gave you confidence and something to hang your hat on when you realized you had a talent for swim. In the beginning, our connection was undeniable. Your sarcasm, quick wit, and easy smile made it easy. As the years went by, the rollers were a bit bigger and lasted longer. The descents never seemed to last long enough. Another roller was waiting for you on the horizon. Another chance to learn about yourself. To learn more about the strength that lies inside you.

You have faced many challenges, but strangely enough, I think swim has helped you find your purpose, discover your talents, and connect with people. I'm confident that in the future when you see a roller, you'll put your head down and work hard to get to the top, knowing you'll have a fun descent waiting for you on the other side.

fleen

❖ **The Sunday Brunch** ❖
Isabel C

Who doesn't like a Sunday brunch? The mind conjures up an array of thoughts the minute you hear brunch: sleeping in, eating a variety of feel-good foods, dressing up in style, and taking the day as it comes. Isabel you are the epitome of Sunday brunch.

Four short years ago you walked on deck not knowing many people or what exactly was happening. You quickly and inauspiciously found your groove. Swim became something you were good at. You fit in so well and connected easily with everyone, yet there was a side of you that didn't scream 'high school girl.' In the midst of screaming teenagers, competition-infused energy, and raging hormones, your calm nature and easy smile were a gentle breeze that defied logic. As the years passed you morphed from obscure contributor to confident leader without fanfare.

This is what I love about you. You are smart, funny, know what you want, and have this quiet yet intense drive to succeed. You absolutely know who you are and what you want. Your style is refreshingly confident and sophisticated, your demeanor is smooth and directed, and your personality is unique and grounded. I have no doubt that you will apply the lessons you learned in high school and swim and use them to continue to guide your path.

Ironically, as you prepare to go to college in Georgia, it wouldn't be a stretch to imagine you there, where hospitality reigns, sitting on a patio enjoying a quiet Sunday brunch. You would naturally be dressed like no one else, hair dyed, taking your sweet time, possessing a maturity beyond your years (which is one of the reasons I affectionately called you "Grandma"), and smiling that easy smile. Taking the day as it comes.

fleen

❖ **The Truth** ❖
Stephanie H

I never know who will walk into my room and tell me they want to swim. I've seen kids who were so excited to join, who never showed up. I've heard stories about growing up in a pool only to find out they can barely float. What was unique about you was you told me the truth.

To say you actually told me the truth is a little like saying Michael Phelps has webbed feet. He actually doesn't, he's just fast. You didn't actually say the words, you just showed me the words. Honestly, I think it was two years before I heard you say anything. In a world where people can say anything and prove nothing, you said nothing and proved everything. This is your truth.

Each year you came back, worked hard, and got a little better. I'm sure there were times when you questioned your reasons why, everyone has them. It was your actions that told the truth. You kept coming back and slowly found friends, your talent, and your purpose.

Fast forward to this year. I can think of two meets that we don't win if you didn't perform. The truth is you are dependable, talented, kind, a great teammate, and an honest soul. This is your truth.

fleen

❖ The Opportunity ❖
Gillian M

Life is like a train. Sometimes that trains speeds down the track while at other times it moves slowly and methodically. We have the opportunity to get on that train at many points in our lives, particularly in high school. One of the things I have admired about you these past four years is your desire to take advantage of the opportunities you've been presented.

I'm always impressed by students when they choose their future. While others have let indecision and doubt choose their path, I have witnessed you set a goal, stay focused in the storm, and realize the prize. I have seen you do this consistently. Academically you have challenged yourself, chosen to put your best foot forward, and reaped the rewards of your efforts. I'm confident you will do the same in college. You have balanced the rigors of music and sports without blinking an eye. While I have noticed the stress of trying to "do it all" in others, I have never once seen it in you. You have remained steadfast in the pursuit of your passions in the midst of tired eyes, tired body, and tired soul. Now here you are on the brink of four more years of the same.

You have discovered your talents and treasures. While singing and dancing might not be some of them, the ones that matter are the ones that will allow you to take advantage of the opportunities that lie ahead. Thank you for the opportunity to be your coach and a witness these past four years

fleen

❖ **The Mall** ❖
Angela I

Full disclosure, I really don't like shopping. I mean I REALLY don't like shopping. All that walking, it's exhausting. If I'm going to shop, I want it all in the same place. That way it's a little less painful. Don't get me wrong, I see some nice things when I shop, but I can't possibly buy everything. You, Angela I, are a one-stop shop. You are a Mall. I have been constantly impressed by the shops in your Mall over the last four years.

The first store I noticed was the "Character Store." In there I found shelves full of selflessness, kindness, and integrity. If anything needed to be done, you were always the first to volunteer. Often I didn't say anything, you saw the need and took care of it. There wasn't a need you didn't like. It got to the point that when I asked for someone to take care of something, I had to tell you you couldn't do it. There isn't a teacher, coach, or teammate who didn't appreciate your willingness to consistently do the right thing or make the right choice.

I walked by "The Comedy Shop" next. You're like the joker. A smile is never far from your face. I am so grateful for your positive outlook, quick wit, and easy laugh. I think everyone who shopped there felt the same way. If they walked in sad, they left energetically happy.

"The T & D Shop" impressed me the most. You don't often find that combination of **T**alent and **D**etermination in a person. It is the rare person who can do just about anything. Yet this was you. It didn't matter if it was athletic or academic, you seamlessly rose to the top in every area.

I know I'm not the only one who wishes they could shop in stores like that all the time. I'm pretty sure in the future the stores in your Mall will continue to have more and more inventory.

fleen

❖ The Curveball ❖
Sam R

The nice thing about some people is their unpredictability. Just when you think you know someone they throw you a curveball. The proverbial 'I did not see that one coming.' Some high school kids fall into the black hole of routine and don't even realize they are there. You, on the other hand, are a breath of fresh air.

My impression of you this year is much different than a year ago. It wasn't that I had a bad impression, I just felt I didn't know you that well. This year I have seen you in so many different ways. All of them positive. There is the enthusiast, the person who is in the middle of everything and many times the instigator: cheering, yelling, and encouraging others. These are amazing lifelong qualities. There is the dancer. The first time I saw it I thought "that is organized chaos." You fueled the audience and the audience fueled you. There is the determinator. Your work ethic and desire to get better is contagious. Knowing that someone wants to be better is what matters most to a coach and you were that person. The listener. I always had the impression that during my "mini pep talks," you were actively engaged and truly listening. You were clearly tuned in, not tuned out.

Thank you for keeping the guys inspired, the girls laughing, and me encouraged.

fleen

Chapter Nineteen

2019

Dear Friends,

Sports… the final frontier. Well, I don't know if swim would be considered the final frontier, but it certainly is a step in that direction. Each year new and returning swimmers begin a journey. Many times they have an idea of what they are about to undertake, but the reality is most of the time it turns out quite different. This year was no exception. Returners made tremendous improvements, new ones surprised themselves and everyone around them, and the coaches had front row seats to it all.

The was a new configuration of schools comprising the Desert Valley League. Out were the schools we have seen for the last 27 years and in were schools we

knew little or nothing about. While the opponents'
faces may have changed, what hadn't changed was
the energy and enthusiasm shown by Cathedral City
swimmers. You wouldn't have known any difference
in the spirit shown by the Lions. Meets were still
a can't miss event, cheering was as important as
swimming, and sportsmanship reigned supreme.

Due to some scheduling confusion, the Lions only
swam 8 times. The girls finished 6-2 and the boys
2-6. The JV Girls were extremely proud of their 7-1
record. Victoria A, Melanie V, and Anahi H were
a few of the many mainstays for the JV Girls. The
Varsity Girls were led by junior CIF qualifiers Jackie
"Bling Bling" L and Kenna I. 2nd year swimmer
Tania R showed the most significant improvement
out of anyone all year. She seemed to get better and
better as the season wore on. Even putting herself in
a position to almost qualify for CIF in the 100 Back.
Seniors Tessa R and Sara A happily completed their
4th year with steady and valuable contributions.
Everyone was especially happy for Sara. During
the summer Sara was diagnosed with leukemia.
The news shook everyone. Through the support of
family and friends, her goal was to complete her
treatment in time for swim season. She did just
that. At the beginning of the season she was a shell of

her former self, but was just happy to be in the pool with a renewed focus of working hard at swimming and having fun. She did just that as she swam the anchor on the CIF qualifying 400 Free Relay. The boys were cursed again by low numbers, but not low talent. Juniors Bernardo N and Jesus V along with sophomore Orion M would dominate races all season long. Losing only a few times all season.

DVL Championships were won by Kenna I in the 100 Breast, Bernardo N the 100 Back, and Jesus V in the 200 Free. Jesus V and Bernardo N combined with Orion M and freshman Richie D to claim the 400 Free relay title. Numerous other athletes would finish in the top 3.

It seemed like another amazing transformation for the Lions from beginning to end. The present and future, as usual, are in good hands.

Swimmingly

❖ **The Seasons** ❖
Sara A

The changing seasons. It's one of the things I enjoy most about nature, the idea that a change is coming. Colors & smells tell us something new has either come back or gone away. Even though we know it's coming, we are often surprised at its intensity, wonder, and beauty. Most people see the changes in their life and can anticipate the effects. And then sometimes we cannot.

High school is a bit like the four seasons. When you were a freshman I remember thinking 'this girl is young.' And by young I meant innocent, naïve, and funny, but not on purpose funny. I thought you were sweet, kind, caring, and dedicated to what you were doing. As the season went on I really appreciated all those qualities. No more so than on the spring break trip. You were the only freshman surrounded by eleven hilarious girls who worked and laughed hard, napped just as hard, consumed any kind of food, and could turn any moment into a memory. It was on this trip, this first season of your high school experience, that I learned three things about you. 1. You are open to anything. I've never laughed so hard as when you ate mussels for the first time. Every part of your mouth, tongue, teeth, and face seemed confused. Which is probably why you started crying. 2. Your command of the English language is suspect at best. To remind you, the fish is called

Cod, not Code. 3. You are more ferocious than any of us knew.

The next few seasons were filled with different weather, different memories. Gone were the early hours and late nights in Palm Springs. Those were replaced by a shiny new facility on campus. Gone also were the spring break trips. Those were replaced by local workouts and activities. What hadn't changed were the three things I learned about you in that first season.

No one could anticipate the weather changes of your last season. Leukemia. When I found out my heart sank. I felt helpless. That kind of season happened to people I didn't know, not to people I knew and cared about. Then I remembered the three things I learned about you in that first season. 1. You are open to anything. Your innocence and naivety worked well as you went through different stages of treatment. 2. Your command of the English language is suspect at best. When I asked you about updates and procedures I didn't understand much of your explanations, and I KNOW that stuff. 3. You are more ferocious than any of us knew. Through it all, you had the most amazing attitude about each day. You didn't let it define you or your future. You were never defeatist or <u>sullen</u> (look it up ;-).

I could not be more proud to have met and coached you. Know that I have probably learned more from you than you'll ever know, about life and about seasons.

fleen

❖ The Attitude ❖
Citlali M

What is the saying? Life is 10% what happens to you and 90% how you react to it. When you stop and think about it, it's really not that far from the truth. All of us know there is one thing we can always count on, and no it's not death and taxes, it's change. Even though we know it's coming, many times we are still surprised, still confused, and often disappointed. But should we be? Our heads say no, but the rest of us sometimes says yes. You on the other hand are an anomaly. 90% of how I see you interact with life each day is so positive that I don't think I've ever noticed the other 10%

In the relatively short time that I have known you, I've seen nothing but commitment, drive, desire, and perspective. Like the colors of the rainbow we are all wonderfully and uniquely made, have strengths and weaknesses, and what we do with those is a daily choice. I love the way you carry yourself with such confidence. You know who you are, what you want to do, and what you can do. A smile or kind word is never far from you. Sports are about connection, not perfection. We try something, we work at it, we do our best, then we go hang with our friends and have some more fun. You've seamlessly incorporated all of those into swim. You're one of the many reasons I want everyone to be a part of my program.

I'm picturing those same qualities carrying you to an incredible future. I would hope that swim has been a small part of creating the amazing person you've become and are becoming. Having already developed such a positive 90%, the next phase of your life should be a piece of cake.

fleen

❖ **The Optimist** ❖
Tessa R

People are often a product of something: family, friends, experiences, etc. All of these things and more create the monster that is us. It's like gas in a car or food in us. As the saying goes, 'what you put in is what you get out.' Because we are a product of our circumstances, it's the view we take towards everything we see that makes us either happy/sad, good/bad, or positive/negative. One of the qualities I saw in you as a freshman that shines brightly to this day is that you are an optimist. You see the happy, good, and positive in everything.

Your freshman year there were so many things that were new, challenging, and rewarding. The schedule, the workouts, the people, and the coaches were all entities orbiting your universe like a tornado. Yet there you were giving it your absolute all, full speed ahead. Sometimes in the wrong direction, but full speed ahead nonetheless. Some of my favorite moments were when you realized these well-intentioned, but misguided moments. They were often met with the face of thoughtfulness, then an "oh yeah, ok." Then full speed ahead again.

Ironically enough the next three years were met with more of the same. Those moments were still funny as ever but showed how genuine you truly are. Only now you were the one demonstrating, the one encouraging, the one leading. These moments only made me more proud of the person you were becoming. The passion you carried with you shone brightly to everyone around. You became the epitome of everything the program stands for: tradition, academics, commitment, character, and most importantly fun.

As kids graduate and begin the next chapter of their lives, it's the lessons learned daily that shape and mold them. We all know we will experience failure, success and everything in between. When you have the attitude of perseverance and gratefulness woven between your failures, successes, and everything in between, the world is your oyster. Tessa, because you are the optimist, the one who sees the happy, good, and positive in everything, you are also the one with the brightest future.

fleen

Chapter Twenty

2020

In 2019 I decided to retire from coaching. I was also involuntarily transferred to an elementary school. The pandemic became the headline for the year. Classes were suspended and schools closed. When I stopped coaching I knew there would be fourteen seniors the following year. One of the first questions I received from athletes and parents was if I was going to write letters to them. In my mind the answer was no. Whoever was going to replace me would establish their own traditions. It turns out the coaching responsibility went to my previous two assistant coaches. Their season was cut short by COVD 19 and any year-end festivities were not allowed. One week before the end of the school year I was talking to my wife about how so much had been taken away from these kids their senior year. She knew exactly what I was going to do next. That day I decided I would write letters to all fourteen. The following week the other coaches and a few athletes followed me as I went house to house and read each letter to each student/athlete. Socially distanced of course.

❖ **The Desire** ❖
Alberto G

A reputation should be a guarded quality. The funny thing about a reputation is it isn't what you think of yourself, it's what others think of you. Your actions determine this on a daily basis. We all wonder at some point what people will say about us. What words will they use to describe us? One word I would use to describe you is desire.

When you started swim, I think you found out pretty quickly that it was not easy. The other side of the pool seemed so close, yet so far. Why is it taking me so long to get there!? Others were so much faster. Well everyone feels this way sooner or later. You want to be the faster one everyone is talking about. To me, it starts with desire.

I first noticed this about you in the classroom. As part of HEAL, it was a desire of yours to be a part of something that could create a positive future. It was not easy at times, but your desire to be there got you through. HEAL offered so much more than just information. It offered acceptance and connection. I think swim for you was very similar. When those two qualities are a part of the experience, it doesn't matter where you start. You just have to have the desire to be there. That is why swim was important to you. Because of your desire, you were accepted and formed connections. It made the whole experience worth it.

You will have many memories to take with you as a result: eating goggles, belly flop dives, food in your face, dancing, and most importantly, fun. Your desire also helped you improve. When you look back at swim and remember your best times, you'll wonder "how was I ever that slow!". Desire made you that way. Desire will also lead your path in the future.

fleen

❖ **The Silly String** ❖
Alondra V

We all went to parties when we were kids. They were good times for sure. Games, lots of really unhealthy food, sometimes gifts, and hanging with friends, what could be better? I'll tell you what could be better: silly string. Some of my fondest party memories as a kid, and as an adult, involved silly string. It is so simple yet so fun. You Alondra, are silly string.

When I started coaching swim, we were not good. We didn't have a lot of swimmers, the ones we had couldn't swim very well, and we did not win anything. Not a meet, not even a race. I knew early on that I needed to do something to make the swimmers want to come back the next day. After thinking about it for a long time (2 seconds), my solution was to increase the fun factor. My logic was that if we weren't going to be Olympic swimmers, we might as well have Olympic level fun.

The day you decided to swim was a memorable day for me. You had this huge smile and laugh to match. Everything was funny. I knew right then I could never be mad at you. Even if I tried it would always end up in laughter. Your energy was infectious, and your fun factor was off the charts. You are the perfect teammate. Cheering, smiling, encouraging others, singing, dancing, you could do it all. As a coach, these are my kind of people. Every team needs a silly string. Someone to remind us all that everything will be OK.

Thank you for being yourself and helping to bring out the best in others.

fleen

❖ The Spirit ❖
Angelica B

So much of swim happens outside the water. When I look back at teams and swimmers, it is the rare occurrence that I remember achievements. Achievements are moments in time that have a short life span. What I remember most are the funny moments, the smiling, faces, and the stories shared by swimmers that will never be forgotten. What I also remember is the spirit of people. I will always remember the spirit of you.

Clearly swim for you was a family affair. I must have met you when all you cared about was climbing the trees at the swim center. Watching your sister swim was secondary. Fast forward to high school and there you were. Another Bustos (meant in a good way), the same yet very different. From my perspective, you are the most expressive Bustos. Your energy is infectious and your spirit contagious. I realize those probably aren't the PC adjectives to use in these corona times, but to me, they fit.

I think swim for you also meant family. I watched you embody the spirit of swim early. You cared about your contributions, you cared about the success of others. and you cared about the legacy of swim. The entire experience felt like a release from normal life for you. You were involved in many things and swim seemed a kind of refuge for you, a place you could either spend or, in many cases, find energy. If you arrived at the pool exhausted from a long day, you left renewed and at peace.

It is always people like you who also renew my energy and my spirit. Thank you for giving all of yourself to swim.

fleen

❖ **The Drive** ❖
Bunnie C

It is day one of your life and you're asked to make a list of all the adjectives you would like others to say about you. Let's ignore the obvious fact that you can neither read, write, or carry on a conversation. At some point, we all become old enough to create our own character, our own reputation. We cannot make our own list of adjectives. What we can do is live our lives in such a way that others identify us with positive adjectives. Out of the many positive adjectives I would use to describe you, the one I like the most is driven.

I will never forget your introduction to polo that first year. You were like many who had never played the game and struggled with swimming. I remember others watching you and wondering if you were going to be ok. Some thought the struggle might be too much for you after a few days. I on the other hand did not share the same sentiment. I saw something else. I saw a person who knew their limitations, but also someone who would not quit. I loved your desire to want to get better. We don't all start or end at the same

317

place. For some, it takes a long time to realize the person they are today will not be the same person in a day, a week, or a month from now. You knew this early, which in my mind, made you enjoy it more. As a coach that is exactly the type of athlete you want on your team. You were not only inspiring to me, but you also inspired others by how driven you were each day in practice. I saw that same spirit in your attitude towards school and how you interacted with others.

In your own quiet way, you were an incredible inspiration to many by the way you attacked each day. While it might not have looked smooth all the time, it definitely made others think about whether they were giving it their all. What an amazing quality to take with you.

fleen

❖ **The Bloomer** ❖
Esteban V

There is nothing better than springtime. After a long winter of seeing little color in nature, spring ushers in a whole new flash of brilliance, a new spectacle of colors, and a new perspective on well…everything. It can be breathtaking and remind us of something brewing from essentially nothing. You Esteban are a bloomer.

When you began swimming you were like most, eager, energetic, raw, and unpolished. You definitely hadn't bloomed yet. Lane 12 was your home. It felt barren, lifeless at times, and seemed like miles away from anything capable of supporting life. Lane 1 might as well have been Hawaii because lane 12 felt like Siberia. Yet there you were learning, working, and trying to get better. I saw your struggle. I've seen it many times before. I've also seen lane 12 bloom in the springtime. I knew this would happen to you at some point. I was just waiting for you to believe it.

I was so excited for you in the middle of your junior year. You had some goal times you were trying to reach, and you were getting closer and closer. Your springtime was coming, you were about to bloom. More importantly, you were starting to represent the essence of swim. Having fun, working hard, and being excited about other swimmers' performances as much or more than your own. That is when I knew you were planting the right seeds.

Then a strange thing happened. A drought came in the form of a virus and cut short another opportunity to bloom. While I'm sure you are disappointed, be happy knowing it would have happened again. This time even more brilliant and spectacular than the last time.

fleen

❖ **The Reflection** ❖
Jackie L

I consider it an honor to write these letters for swim seniors. Some of these letters write themselves. Others take time. All are written because of the deep appreciation I feel to have coached such quality student/athletes. You are one of the special ones.

I remember when you joined. You 'kinda' knew what was happening, most of the time anyway, but just went with the flow regardless. I could see early on that you possessed the ability to want to be the best version of yourself. Not the best swimmer or best polo player, but the best version of you. Many people play sports in high school, but it is a select few who realize the competition is not across the pool, it is within. It is this realization that fuels athletes like you. I truly believe you became the accomplished athlete you are because you cared about the quality of your effort. It was not about your level of talent or my coaching. I truly believe your light shined bright because you wanted to be the best version of you.

It is exciting to see student-athletes like you reflect in such a positive way. Teammates could also tell there was something special about the way you practiced, competed, encouraged others, and committed to being the best student possible. Each year I could see the internal struggle. I could see the self-reflection. You never blamed me, or others, for your performance. You only wanted to improve. After all, isn't improvement what we should all be striving for?

I am sad your final year was cut short. I know you had aspirations for yourself and for your team. Be content in the knowledge that your motivation came from a good place. From a selfless place. I am beyond thrilled for you and what lies ahead. You will have challenges for sure, but I am confident you will be a shining star. That light will guide, not only your path but the paths of others.

fleen

❖ **The Discovery** ❖
Jesus V

Who doesn't like to find something new like $5 hiding in your pocket, the moment you finally understand something in Math or the coolest new video on Instagram, Facebook, YouTube, Snapchat, TikTok, etc, etc. Think about it, discovery is the foundation of pretty much everything. It is one of the things I love most about being a coach. I get to witness kids discover so much about themselves every single year, and I'm not just talking about swimming ability.

One of my priorities as a coach has always been to make sure my athletes enjoy the experience and discover something about themselves. Some will discover a hidden athletic talent and excel, like you. Some will discover new friends that will become lifelong friends, like you. Some will discover newfound confidence that not only helps them in the pool, but also in the classroom, like you. Some will discover that they were capable of more than they ever thought possible, like you. Finally, some will discover that the journey is far more important than the destination, like you.

When you began swim, I could see you were not like most. You had this amazing ability to connect. Yeah, you wanted to get better, but fun was at the forefront of your priorities. People were at the forefront. To me, that's how it should be. In time, athletes will discover they have the ability and will match that with effort in the pool. Ultimately you discovered this quality about yourself. We all soon learned that when the lights were the brightest, you shined the most. What we also noticed was if it went well, great, if it didn't go well, that was OK too.

To witness this type of growth is what I love about coaching. There is so much more to swim than practice and competition. When athletes like you discover this early, they enjoy it more and use the experience to prepare them for life after high school. I'm pretty sure you discovered many incredibly positive things about yourself in swim. Use those discoveries to create your future. I'm sure you will like what you find.

fleen

❖ **The Choice** ❖
Kassandra R

Think about all the choices we make in a day. I know that may seem a bit overwhelming. The minute we wake up we start. In fact, that first choice is 'get up.' It just seems to snowball from there. We don't have time to think through all our decisions in a day, just a select 1000, give or take a few. We have to rely on our instinct to guide us. That internal voice that seems to know just what to think, say or do. Like an invisible friend on our shoulder telling us 'NOOOOO!!' or 'GO FOR IT!!! As a coach, I don't have the energy to obsess over all the choices my athletes make. I try to focus on one: 'Do you want to swim?'

When you chose to swim, I knew little about you. I was just thrilled another person chose to be a part of the program. I could see you were eager, enthusiastic, athletic, and motivated. That was enough for me. I could see you fit in well with the others. That made me smile. It was fun to see you eat your goggles every now and then, wear a pie on your face with a smile, and see you improve each week.

The thing that defines us is not one decision, but the totality of the choices we make over time. I am about as far from perfect as one can get. I can barely make out the 'perfect' sign with my eyes. This is probably why I feel it is important to take a well-rounded approach to life. Full steam ahead, but with the ability to notice the caution signs off to each side. I understand high school is sometimes difficult to navigate. Choices made, while not always good, are well-intentioned.

You are an amazing, happy, smiling, talented, good-natured soul. Focus on these strengths and the many others you possess to help you make the best choices possible moving forward. I am so thankful for all the positive contributions you have given swim over the last three years. I am disappointed your last hoorah was taken from you. I am also disappointed I could not witness the myriad of positive choices you would have made this year.

fleen

❖ **The Amalgamation** ❖
Kathelinne R

We are a product of all we do and should not be defined by our successes nor our failures. We are imperfect people navigating an imperfect world. In some ways, high school is the training ground for our future. Looking back we hardly recognize the bright-eyed, anxiety-filled freshman we once were. In many ways, we were just winging it. We thought we knew better, but we're really just doing our best while being flooded with emotions, people, and experiences. One of the things I appreciated about you was your sincerity of spirit.

As a freshman, you quickly became unforgettable. In class, around campus, and in the pool, a smile was never far from your face. Fun was always just around the corner. If it wasn't there, you just went around another corner. We clicked because sarcasm was our middle name. We each took what we did seriously, but not ourselves. You with your school work and commitment to aquatics and me with teaching and coaching. It was fun for me to see you become involved and learn over the course of your high school experience. If things didn't go well, it wasn't the end of the world. You just tried it again. After all, tomorrow was just waiting around the corner.

When I look at you now I don't see that bright-eyed, anxiety-filled freshman. I see a person living in the moment. I see a person immersing themselves in the experiences before them. I see a person learning, living, and looking to take advantage of the next sarcastic opportunity.

We do not all make perfect decisions. I would like to think most of us have good intentions. I have no doubt your intentions are good. As you move on from here, know that I will always believe in you. You are nowhere near the end of your journey. Remember you are an amalgamation of your successes <u>and</u> your failures and will continue to be. Remember also that something fun is always waiting for you around the corner. Make the most of it.

fleen

❖ **The Redirect** ❖
Kenna I

I remember it like it was yesterday. Your sister introduced us. I started the conversation by asking simple questions. What do you like to do? What are you interested in? Do you like swimming? Are you planning to be a part of the HEAL Academy? In your biggest most sincerely confident/arrogant 8ᵗʰ grade manner, you answered: Nothing. Nothing. No. I'm going to the culinary academy at Rancho. "That's great" I remember saying. Later I mentioned to your sister that you seemed pretty sure of your direction. She responded with "I guess." Imagine my surprise when I found out you were accepted into the HEAL Academy. (picture a sideways smile on my face). Swim still wasn't on the table, but as we both knew, that would also change. To this day I don't know what changed in you. I'm just grateful it did.

As far as I knew, you did not have a treasure chest full of athletic experience. Perfect I thought. You'll be just like everyone else. What I saw in you was a desire to be good, to be better. What I did not see was your sneaky competitive nature. It fueled you in music, it fueled you in school, and it ultimately fueled you in swim.

That first year you were like many in the 'humble beginning' phase. Even at that point, I noticed four things in you that made me smile and have faith in you. You worked, you had fun, you were a fantastic teammate, and you improved. Every time a challenge was presented to you, you embraced each with a determined grace. No obstacle was too great.

The most enjoyable moment as a coach is when an athlete sees what they can become. That first year, CIF might well have been the ancient pyramids of Egypt. That trip was for somebody else. I felt like your travel agent. I made plans and charted your course. You did the rest. I was so happy for you.

While your last year was taken from_you, it won't diminish the lessons you'll take with you. The most important of which is that anything is possible with the right attitude.

fleen

❖ The Willing ❖
Natalie G

Eyes wide open is definitely a good philosophy of life. That way you can see all the possibilities before you. That philosophy is never more important than in high school. For the first time, you are presented with numerous opportunities to become involved. All it takes is a willingness to take the first step. One of the things I noticed about you right away is that you were always willing to take that step.

I love old two-story wooden cabins. There are many in Oregon where I grew up. Places full of old stories and rickety staircases that kept the fear factor and imagination fresh. It became a game to try and walk around without causing the floors or steps to creak. You never knew if the next step would be able to support you or if you'd fall right through. You had to be willing to try. Sometimes it held, sometimes it didn't, but you couldn't let fear stop you.

Throughout high school, you were willing to experience many things. Whether athletic or HEAL related, you consistently made the willing choice to try. Not knowing if the experience would support you, you tried anyway. Because of this you had the chance to see and do so many things that have shaped you as a person. The byproduct of having that willingness to try has been an increased self-confidence, academic, and athletic achievement, communication skills, organization, problem-solving, and way too many laughable moments to count.

I'll always remember you being the one willing to lead, encourage, work, suffer, and commit to all things swim. Your willingness has given you so much more to remember than most. It will also be the guiding light you will use to navigate an uncertain future in uncertain times.

fleen

❖ **The Prospect** ❖
Tania R

As Forest Gump said "life is like a box of chocolates, you never know what you are going to get." As a coach that is my introduction to every new season. I never know what I am going to get. Faces I don't know full of energy that won't quit and talent waiting to be discovered. The unique thing about you was that I saw something in you early. I could see a prospect. The only issue was you couldn't see it in yourself. Yet.

You became involved, but it always felt like you were dipping one toe in the water, unsure if you wanted to go all in. Would the water be too uncomfortable? Would I even enjoy the effort it would take? Then something happened that I've seen many times over. You finally saw something in yourself. You started to improve and that seemed to fuel the fire. The little things about each practice and competition were met with a newfound energy. You smiled easier, worked harder, and became a voice people listened to. Your results spoke for themselves. You started to become the person I saw two years ago. You blossomed.

Then suddenly you had it all taken away your Senior year. No one saw it coming. No one knew what would happen day to day. Suddenly all the things you saw for yourself were taken away. The fire that began to burn in swim, was unexpectedly blown out. It's funny the lessons you learn when your world is turned upside down. The 'I can't wait' abruptly became the "I wonder what would have been.' I hope you take with you a newfound sense of confidence. You have so much going for you. Your talents are still under the surface waiting to be unveiled. They may not be connected to swim. Continue to see in yourself the wonderful things some of us have always seen.

fleen

❖ **The Product** ❖
Bernardo N

Life can sometimes be an uncertain challenge. It is not always easy, but it is definitely worth the effort. As most of us know, what you put in is what you get out. Or as I prefer to say: 'process produces product.' The product for many is not always clear. That makes the process the challenge. Why should I put in the work for an uncertain product? In three short years, you have made it a priority to put yourself through the 'process' even though the product was unclear.

When you began swimming, I don't know if you really knew where you were going. So much of swim is the entirety of the experience. Team meals, getting cool stuff, practicing, competing with friends new and old, Do The Trick, and shaving parties. Those alone are pretty cool products. But the essence of swim is competition and improvement. That being said, everyone will have a different product at the end.

When you began, I did not know exactly what your product would look like. All I knew was you were positive, committed, and fun to coach. That was all I needed. Then you started to show glimpses of awesomeness, followed up by even more glimpses of awesomeness. Your times improved, but more importantly, your work ethic began to match your desire to be better. That concept is difficult for many to understand. They want success the easy way, but we all know that is not possible.

You went from unnoticed freshman to DVL Champion in three short years. Then fate stepped in and prevented you from taking the next step, CIF. What makes me proud is not only your achievement but your dedication to the process. During your time in swim you also grew to be a great teammate, leader, and person. Ultimately those are the qualities that determine your future, not a DVL title. Be proud of your accomplishments as an athlete, be more proud of your accomplishments as a person.

fleen

Chapter Twenty-one

The Early Years

❖ **The Passion** ❖
Brad M '96

Passion is a word many of us would like attached to us, yet many don't. The question then becomes, why? Why do some have it and others only wish they had it? While not an easy question to answer, the truth lies in the action. There is 'talking about it' and 'being about it'. You, Brad Morris, have lived a life of 'being about it'.

Our paths crossed in middle school. You were the chubby guy who was nice to everyone, loved talking about his grandfather, and learned to play golf as a result. Our paths crossed again in high school. The chubby guy had morphed into a slimmer frame and tried other sports, including baseball. What hadn't changed was his passion. A passion for sports, people, and adventure was clearly evident. Whether rollerblading, watching X-Files, or spending time with family and friends, passion was part of your daily fabric.

Our paths crossed again your sophomore year when you made a decision to swim. Neither of us at the time would know the impact your passion would have on both our lives. We were both relatively new to the sport. What wasn't new was your passion for life. That passion was backed by an incredible work ethic, dedication, commitment, and trust. I don't think you realized at the time how much your passion fueled me to be the best coach possible. I am still amazed at how much you accomplished in 3 short years. Not just the accolades, but the positive impression you left on so many lives, including my own. You and the other athletes of your generation taught me sports was more about passion than performance. The concept of family was solidified in me and is something that has continued to separate my program from every other program.

The success you had after high school was no surprise to me. With passion as your guide, you continued to excel and lead others. Even today, I have seen this to be your truth. You have continued to 'be about it' in every aspect of your life. I am thankful to have witnessed your journey all these years later and even luckier to be able to call you friend.

fleen

❖ **The First** ❖
Laina H '97

History is really only made once. Each time after that, it can only repeat itself. There is something about laying the foundation that cements a legacy. Not many people get to be the first. You, Laina, had many firsts.

When I look back I think how lucky I was to be blessed with you. You were a talented swimmer, a superior student, a willing participant, and a caring soul. As a coach in training, I just tried not to mess you up. I wanted to make sure you had fun, felt included, and understood the meaning of what would eventually be called Lion Pride. On all accounts, you thrived.

You were the first to represent Cathedral City at CIF. I honestly felt more like a fan than a coach. Four short years, and many accolades later, you were part of the school's first and only CIF Championship. From team meals to cheers to new traditions, you were a part of all those firsts too.

As a person, you were the one who others looked to first for how to work hard, how to dedicate yourself in the pool and the classroom, and how to do it all with a smile on your face.

Perhaps your greatest quality was your ability to include everyone and make them feel important. I include myself in that group. Whether they could swim a little or barely at all, you made them feel included. A smile, a word of encouragement, or one of your super-strong hugs was all it took.

Talent comes and goes, but it is who we are as people, that is what we will remember. You will be remembered for many firsts throughout your time at Cathedral City. Be happy knowing that you will be remembered for many of your swimming accomplishments, but be at peace knowing that you will be known for who you were as a person first.

fleen

❖ **The Tattoo** ❖
Lindsay P '95

The laugh. The personality. The one eye twinge. The energy. The encourager. The prankster. The young girl who immersed herself in school to overcome everything outside of school. I remember them all. Like a tattoo, you have left an indelible mark on many people over the years. I am thankful to be one of them.

While we can't always explain the choices we make and the life we are given, we can move forward. As I look back, I remember many moments where you did just that. You moved forward. That is honestly one of the reasons I knew you would become who you are today and why I would never forget you.

My moments may surprise you. I remember you helping me arrange my classroom upon returning to school one summer. I think we both missed each other and were just happy to laugh together again. I remember you teasing Ned and him trying unsuccessfully to be cool about it. I remember the pained look on your face after a tough set and I remember the energy you still had to do a back-flip later. I remember the look on your face when you made it to CIF your senior year and I remember the joy I felt when I saw your name on the list. I remember the moments you shared your struggles and the helplessness I felt inside. I think it was at that first moment, you simply helping me arrange my classroom, that I knew I would never forget you.

We started together, you as a student-athlete and me as a coach. Neither one of us knew exactly what we were doing, but for some odd reason, we fully believed and trusted each other.

I can't explain why swimming at Cathedral City has become more than a sport, but I do know you are one of the main reasons. I can't reason why you have left such a lasting impression on me, but I can tell you I am grateful. I can't begin to tell you how proud I am of the woman you have become, but I can tell you I am not surprised.

fleen

❖ The Alarm ❖
Amy S '97

Because it was done with the club team before I arrived, I thought it was something most teams did. I wasn't a swimmer growing up so the idea of 5 am morning practices, while crazy in my mind, seemed the thing to do. So when I started coaching the high school team I thought it was something I needed to do as well. The alarm, while not my friend, was something I became used to each morning. What I didn't realize was your alarm did not ring the same time as mine each morning.

I don't even think I knew about it at first. I only remember you being at 5 am morning on time every day. Almost everyone was very faithful in those early years. Worrying about someone being late or not coming was luckily not a major concern. Will Amy show up on time was the farthest thing from my mind. I figured if you swam for the high school, you lived in the area. Then I discovered you lived 45 minutes away. Your father brought you to practice, waited in the car, drove you to school, then he went to work. Then I learned when you were young you were an amazing gymnast only to have that derailed by scoliosis. Swimming became something you could do that didn't exacerbate the problem. The high school near your house didn't offer much in the way of swimming so you were encouraged by age group swim friends to come to my school.

Throughout the years you never complained, weren't negative, nor whined about what you had to go through each day to swim. I was so grateful for your sacrifice and I think you were grateful to be a part of something special. You helped build the program from nothing and were the ideal teammate. Your laugh came as easy as your schoolwork. Your commitment was the envy of everyone. They understood what you had to go through each day to swim. It made their issues seem trivial.

While I'm sure you didn't enjoy hearing that alarm each morning, you should be proud of all the positive decisions you made each day. To think it all started with an alarm.

fleen

❖ **The Kind of** ❖
Ned D '95

Y ou are literally part of the foundation. The year the school was opened there was a swim team. Its competition was basically JV teams. There were no real expectations other than to keep a few kids happy. It was a bit like cooking spaghetti. Throw some noodles on the wall to see what sticks. Then do more of that. There you were in all your inexperienced glory. When I started coaching the next year, the Athletic Director told me there weren't that many kids on the team, and only one "kind of" knew how to swim. You were the "kind of."

I didn't have many expectations at the beginning. Work hard, have fun, and give everyone a reason to come back the next day. After watching everyone swim that first day, I was thrilled to have a "kind of." You could move pretty well through the water. Much better than the others. So naturally, I tried to make you the flyer. It was not pretty and you were not that happy, but you tried. Not pretty, like looking at the beginning of a compost pile not pretty. As a science teacher, I know that compost piles never look or smell that nice in the beginning. The end is another story. The end is what keeps us motivated to endure the beginning. By the time you graduated, you had made some pretty significant contributions.

You saw many changes those last three years. You were naturally an incredible student. Often the work was so easy you weren't too keen on the homework side of school. You soon learned how important detail was, not only in swimming, but also in school. Watching you morph into a leader your senior year was a joy to witness. You had been part of that humble beginning and then as a senior, you were preparing for CIF. All of us will never forget the team dinner we had prior to CIF. Some shaving was happening, but you told us you would do it at home. When we saw you the next day, you had band-aids all over your shins. Apparently you missed the memo about using an electric shaver first, then razoring the rest if you had hairy legs.

It was moments like these and many more that endeared you to everyone. Thank you for jumping on board with all the craziness during those years. Everyone was driving without a rudder and couldn't have been happier. Not many will ever experience the highs and lows like you and not many can say they were part of the foundation. You can proudly say you have literally seen it all. To think, it all started with a "kind of."

fleen

❖ **The Hole** ❖
Lyndee H '98

It was the first time I visited your house. I had known you and your family for about a year when your mom invited me over for dinner. You must have been about 9 or 10 years old. Spending time with people outside of the usual parameters of interacting was always fun for me. So of course the answer was yes. When I walked into your house, you and your sisters were eager to greet me. I had shorts on and, unbeknownst to me, a small hole from my wallet imprint was growing. You noticed and without hesitation grabbed at the hole and basically tore the pocket off. Accidentally of course ;-). There I was, half of the back of my shorts ripped off and my boxers exposed. No one prepares you for moments like that. So I just laughed. This impulsiveness would continue to be a trademark for you.

I still followed you and your sisters after I stopped coaching your club team. You were a record-setting machine. At every Age Group you were one of the top swimmers in Southern California. While that was great, I just enjoyed hanging out with you and your family. Yeah, you were part of a tremendous swimming family, but our times together were just about fun, serious hard fun.

By the time you joined my high school program you had already qualified for Olympic Trials. Again, that was great, but you were still about the fun, good hard fun. You could have gone to the more established swim program at Palm Springs High School, but you chose to come to my school. My program was being built upon working very hard, but also about having huge amounts of fun off the pool deck. You were a perfect fit. No one worked harder than you and no one wanted to have more fun than you. While I marveled at your dedication and talent, I was more enamored with your desire to have fun. A bit like you, I took what I did very seriously, but not myself. We were a perfect fit and the results showed. 7 time CIF Champion, 4 time CIF relay Champion (one relay set a record that stood for 12 years), part of CIF Champion and Runner up Teams, CIF Female Swimmer of the Meet, Arco AM/PM Student-Athlete of the Year, and High School Valedictorian. Next stop, UCLA.

Again, all of those were amazing accomplishments, but I will remember much more about you than your swimming accolades. I'll remember your energetic smile, the way you motivated and included EVERYONE on the team. Also how tired you were on the spring break trips., not so much from training, but from lack of sleep. When I asked why you said it was because you didn't want to miss any fun. You clearly had a bad case of FOMO. I'll remember how much you hated to lose and your incredible time management skills. I never worried about you sacrificing training, school work, family, or friends.

And I will remember your impulsiveness. This trait could have been your downfall, but I think both of us believed in you too much to let it dominate your character for too long. When you argued with your teachers, I believed in you. When you ran away from home during your rebellious phase, I believed in you. When you weren't always nice to people who cared about you, I still believed in you. As we both know, you had a few, as you once put it "correctable moments." Still, I believed in you. Thank you for thinking enough of me to listen to my words of correction and encouragement. I've always considered you more than just an athlete. I consider you a friend for life.

fleen

❖ **The Surfer** ❖
Rugby C '00

I met you after your cousin suggested you try swimming as a way to integrate into an American high school. You were still learning English after arriving from Venezuela. As a champion surfer in your country, swimming seemed the closest thing to surfing in the desert. Other than swimming in the ocean, you had no experience being on a competitive swim team. You started a bit late that first year and we had already completed time trials. I'll never forget when you finally swam your 50 Free time trial. Your time was among the fastest on the team. The funny thing was, you didn't know how to flip turn and you swam as if you were on a surfboard. Your arms were fast and wide with just a hint of a kick. I knew then you would be something special and I was more than happy to be along for the ride.

I remember you being initially very quiet, but when the conversation switched to something that interested you, your mouth and eyes created this huge inviting smile. It was that smile and positive attitude that immediately endeared you to everyone. Your confidence grew along with your personality. We all soon learned you were quite the jokester. You were faux serious one minute then gave a big belly laugh seconds later. You had a Ph.D. in sarcasm. I remember being on the receiving end of it many times.

You were also becoming an incredible swimmer. Your work ethic certainly matched your talent. You were learning strokes faster than most. Freestyle came very easy for you and your times dropped quickly, but it was your breaststroke that surprised us all. You were dropping time every meet. Surprisingly, your first CIF cut would be in the 100 Breast.

While competitive swimming came naturally to you, it was your friendly, hilarious nature that I appreciated most. Our program has more fun in a week than some do in a season and you certainly added to the chaos. You were the best teammate and a ray of sunshine for everyone. On one of our spring break trips to Santa Barbara, I told you to bring your surfboard. When I lived there I also surfed. It was my plan to go surfing with you. That was secretly one of the things I was looking forward to most about the week. While the rest of the team was hanging out on the beach, I took you to one of the spots I used to surf. While the waves weren't great I just remember being amazed at how at ease and comfortable you were on a surfboard. And all the while you were still smiling like a lighthouse with your eyes.

I am grateful for everything my swim program gave to you. I'm even more grateful for everything you gave to the program. You are definitely one of a kind.

fleen

❖ **The Gas Pump** ❖
Lauren F '99

Self starter doesn't even begin to describe you. Ever since I have known you, you have been an organized, driven, dedicated, committed, kind, and most thoughtful teammate and person. Economically speaking, I don't think you have ever been in the red at any point in your life. You were a talented CIF swimmer, school valedictorian, and friend to all. This, is why it was so unusual for you to be late for practice. I wasn't worried, I trusted you, but I had to tilt my head just a little wondering where you were. When you finally arrived just a few minutes late, I asked why. You said you had to get gas for your car and didn't know how to use the pump so you drove to a station that did it for you. I could only smile.

The early years provided some of the most entertaining experiences for me and the entire team. If you weren't willing to spend a lot of time laughing, it might have been strange for you entering the program. When you came in as an incredible swimmer, it only added to the success of the team. You were an invaluable part of some of the most amazingly talented teams in school history. Club swimming tended to focus on results first and fun second. For us, it was the other way around. I think this was a switch for you at the beginning. We had many loud personalities in those years. While you weren't exactly built that way, you soon learned to adapt and enjoy. It was clear you were all in with the team activities, spring break trips, crazy parts of practice, and general frivolity.

As a coach you want everyone in your program to have fun and experience some success. When someone with your pedigree enters, there is always a little pressure to build upon that foundation. My desire is for everyone to be the best version of themselves both as a student/athlete and a person. I was confident in my ability to train talented swimmers, but my challenge was to make sure they had fun being part of a team. You made that very easy for me.

You're everything a coach would want in a student/athlete. Thank you for trusting me. You worked hard and knew that your efforts would be rewarded and they absolutely were as a collegiate swimmer, MVP, and in Law School. With a family of your own now, I'm certain you are an amazing example of what is possible.

fleen

❖ **The Time Trial** ❖
Bobby M '96

Being so new to the whole swim coach world, I didn't always know if I was doing the right things. One of the things I started early was time trials. After a few weeks of instruction, literally teaching people to float and swim, we had time trials. I knew the beginning for most would be less than stellar, but at least I knew their finish would be better. There you were with your skinny arms, legs, fingers, and toes. We had done 100 free time trials the day before and you blasted a 1:16. I will never forget your breaststroke time trial the next day. It was literally the same time. I thought I did something wrong. I double-checked and realized the time was legit. It was then I learned you would be special.

I think you joined swim because you spent a lot of time at the river with your family jet skiing and jumping off bridges. You know, the typical transition to aquatics. Neither one of us knew fully what we were doing each day, but blindly trusted each other as if we did. Turns out, that was the best thing we could have done. We didn't have crazy expectations of winning the League or qualifying for CIF. I think we both just wanted to enjoy the experience. And we definitely did that. Team meals, funny warm-ups and practices, cheering like crazy for everyone, season-ending BBQ sleepovers, even rollerblading through neighborhoods was almost as enjoyable as getting best times.

Yet there you were at the end of your second year getting closer and closer to a CIF cut. I was amazed. Your 1:16 had turned into a 1:06 by season's end. Breaststroke was definitely working for you. Yet each stroke was getting better as well.

At time trials your junior year, your backstroke and breaststroke were literally the same time, 1:09. Your breaststroke was becoming a thing of beauty and your backstroke was becoming a thing of wonder. Wonder, as in "how can he go that fast without a flutter kick?" You just breaststroke kicked your backstroke. I wasn't going to try and change that. I was just happy you didn't breaststroke kick your freestyle. Not only was your breaststroke improving, you were also consistently dropping time in your IM. At the end of the season you still needed a CIF for breaststroke. You had been close so many times, but hadn't qualified. At League Finals you finished 3rd with a 1:03.09 and finally achieved your qualifying time. At CIF you shocked everyone, even myself, by swimming a 1:00.53. This trusting soul, this wonderful teammate, this fun-loving, hard-working athlete was becoming an incredible swimmer.

For some reason you missed time trials your senior year. We'll never know how that year started, but we definitely know how it ended. You didn't lose a race your senior year and won CIF.

As we both know, that would not be the end. You continued to amaze me when you walked on at UNLV, eventually earned a scholarship and ultimately became a team captain. You capped it off by setting school and conference records in the 100 Breast and 200 & 400 Medley Relays. You continued to amaze me when you finished 14th at the 2000 Olympic Trials. You even swam for Team USA. You also won a National Championship Medley Relay with Jason Lezak (8 Olympic medals-4 Gold), Michael Cavick (who infamously lost to Michael Phelps in the 2008 Olympic 100 fly by .01), and Aaron Piersol (7 Olympic medals-5 Gold, world record). FYI, jet skiers who start swimming in High School are not normally supposed to swim on National Championship relays with these people.

All of that and more amazes me. You have consistently given time and resources back to the program you came from, you have created a successful business, you have become a wonderful husband and father to three lovely girls, and that we are still friends to this day.

I don't know your future, but I'm confident the amazement will not end.

fleen

❖ **The Eyes** ❖
Roz M '97

They say the eyes are windows to the soul. For me, they are the most inviting part of a person. I can tell a lot about a person just by looking into their eyes. I'm a firm believer that our eyes can only tell the truth, they cannot lie. Which makes our first encounter, or encounters a bit unusual. I joke that you didn't really look me in the eye until your junior year. You had this propensity to look down at something most of the time those first few years. While unusual at the time, I knew a cherished soul was inside. It just took a few years.

You joined swim and water polo not knowing much about either. Maybe that was the fuel you needed to get started. Playing polo with the boys and swimming on a team dominated by some pretty strong and crazy personalities provided the perfect backdrop for you. As they say, it was literally sink or swim at the start. I remember you trying to understand what was going on, but not really being able to comprehend my explanations. That didn't seem to deter you from dedicating yourself to aquatics. You were all in. Even though I couldn't see it clearly in your eyes yet. You filled those first few years with so much sacrifice. You may have been apprehensive about looking me in the eye, fearing I didn't believe in you. That couldn't have been further from the truth. I was just waiting for your eyes to shine.

Once you started experiencing some success, your eyes showed me everything: struggle, relief, perseverance, and pure joy. I saw you dominating the boys on the way to becoming MVP of the boys' water polo team. I saw you watching your times drop in swim, knowing you were such a huge part of the immediate success of the team. Your eyes showed me that you were sacrificing your personal ambitions at CIF for the good of the team; then swimming faster than you ever had before as part of a CIF Championship team. All the while, your eyes were telling the story of growth and confidence. That confidence led you to college where you were an All-American water polo player and team leader.

I'll never forget your beginning. The shy eyes of a soul waiting to bloom. I'll never forget the end. The soulful eyes of power, grace, and confidence. To this day, I still look forward to seeing you. To look in your eyes and see one of the most amazingly talented souls I've ever had the pleasure of knowing.

fleen

❖ **The Dolphin** ❖
Leslie H '00

We've all seen the beauty, strength, and amazement of dolphins swimming. They are even more spectacular when watching them live. They move effortlessly and gracefully through any type of water, confident with each move, daring in their effortless ease. I've heard people talk about top-level swimmers the same way. How they make it look easy. How they waste no energy in movement How they look like they are not even trying, only to look at the clock and witness another incredible time. You are a dolphin.

I met you when you were 8 or 9 years old. You were funny, fun-loving, and exuberant to a fault. I had just started coaching your club team. (My first swim coaching experience). Even then, watching you swim was eye-opening. Swimming was important, but even then you knew it was also supposed to be fun. Fun was our connection. You knew I raced triathlons and you wanted to try one. I remember running and biking with you, more laughing than training, but I loved it.

Fast forward to high school where I was once again your coach. We never lost contact and I couldn't wait for you to be a part of what was becoming a very accomplished program. Not because you were talented, I knew you would be very successful, mostly because I knew you would bring the fun factor. You are engaging, positive, and everyone's best friend. That's what I looked forward to, the team witnessing the 'Leslie experience.' I could not have been happier. You fit in perfectly and were swimming well and, more importantly, having fun.

Then something happened after your junior year. For some reason, something else became more important than the fun factor in swim. I returned to school that Fall to learn from your friends that you would not be swimming. Snowboarding was your new passion. I didn't completely understand and we did not talk about it. Our season started without you. Then one of your friends asked if it was too late for you to join swim. The door had never been closed and the answer was yes, but I had to hear it from you. I know that conversation was not easy for you. As a coach and someone who had know you for many years, my only concern was that you be happy. I was thrilled we finally met and you shared your feelings and asked if you could return. A quick yes was followed with "you have to promise me you'll do these two things. One, you have to do everything I ask, and two you have to have fun.

The rest of the season was a blur of the "Leslie experience.' You were working hard, swimming well, but most importantly, having fun became the most important thing. The dolphin I had seen for so many years was faster than ever. I know you couldn't see my face when you swam, but my smile could not have been bigger. I was happy you were swimming fast, but I was happier knowing you were having so much fun. It was no surprise to me that you would end up swimming at UCLA as a result. Once fun became the priority, you excelled. To this day you have been the most mesmerizing swimmer for me to watch.

I am so happy to have known you for so many years. You truly made my coaching experience a joy.

fleen

❖ **The Legacy** ❖
Carrie S '99

Many people have ideas. Not many people act on them. Many people think about doing something. Not many people actually do. Many people ask questions. Not many people actively seek answers. I think when we met neither of us knew what kind of person you would be. What both of us did know was neither was just going to settle for the status quo. We would pursue. Your pursuit led to a memorable legacy.

Many kids enter high school trying to survive the daily changes of development. The first step to survival is to get involved. You joined swim and water polo not knowing much about either, but eager to learn. Your desire and work ethic were second to none. Soon you discovered a passion for both sports. We both knew water polo held a special place in your heart. The problem was that a girls program did not exist at the time. For you and a handful of other girls, that didn't matter. If the only option was to play with the boys, then so be it, we'll play with the boys. This is exactly what you all did for three years.

I remember you came into my room sometime during that third year asking what it would take to start a girls' program. You had researched that girl programs were already in place in and around Los Angeles. I said you needed to gauge interest at the other high schools in the league, write letters to their coaches and Athletic Directors, gather the information, and make a proposal to our Athletic Director who would take it from there. They could not deny the program if there was sufficient interest. Finally, I told you I would coach the team if the answer was yes. (At the time I had recently stopped coaching boy's water polo after starting the program because swimming was becoming hugely popular).

Your pursuit of water polo is the reason it exists in our area. Someone had to create the spark. Someone had to care enough to continually fuel the fire. That someone was you. While many dream, you acted. This is your enduring legacy. It would turn out to be one of many enduring legacies you left behind after you graduated. Thank you for pursuing your passions and caring enough to act on them. It is a testament to who you are as a person. It is your legacy.

fleen

DVL - Desert Valley League

CIF - California Interscholastic Federation. The governing body of our post season championship. The equivalent of a state meet.

HEAL - Health and Environmental Academy of Learning. An on campus academy of which Fleener was a founding member. He taught Biology and Anatomy.

AVID - Advancement Via Individual Determination. Another on campus academy.

Printed in the United States
by Baker & Taylor Publisher Services